To LINDA, my wonderful wife
For her enormous assistance and encouragement

For the information mentioned in my book, concerning various people of historical significance, as well as the history of The Bible, with its sundry revisions, I give full credit to The Columbia Encyclopaedia, third edition, and those learned people who contributed to its compilation. I found this book invaluable and remarkable, for the vast amount of knowledge encompassed in its contents.

TO HELL WITH POSITIVE THINKING

by James Moriarty

The next time some clown tells me to 'think positive' I will sorely be tempted to kick him/her squarely where it hurts most! It seems that the civilized world has been over-run by exponents of this Positive Thinking nonsense. Apparently there exists an endless supply of 'experts' appearing on television, extolling its virtues, and urging us to send for their tapes, buy their books, or attend their seminars, invariably held at impressive venues, and charging exorbitant admission prices. Presumably, it must be positively profitable for them, like starting up a new religion! One does wonder however, whether these 'gurus' of positive thinking, (henceforth referred to as P.T.) are the only ones who ultimately benefit, leaving in their wake, a trail of disillusioned, confused souls, who after being effectively brain-washed, go forth into the real world to hit the brick wall of cynicism, deceit and artificiality that awaits them. Why are so many people terrified of being called negative thinkers? It is because these so-called 'positive thinkers' and their brain-dead conformist disciples are conditioned into branding anyone who disagrees with them as 'negative thinkers'! The trendy present-day syndrome among the pseudo-intellectuals is to chant 'Think Positive'. Have these barnacles ever solved any of the world's social or economic problems? Quite the opposite—they have created more! After World War Two we were all led to believe that things would get better. Nuclear power stations and nuclear power were the wonders of the 1950's, and the construction of nuclear power stations became a status symbol of international proportions. Even those smaller countries whose people lived in poverty and suffered privation had to build nuclear installations. Some of the sneakier ones used them to develop nuclear weaponry. Had our scientists and leaders been more negative about nuclear proliferation, we would not be confronted now with the apparently insurmountable problem of nuclear waste disposal, radiation leaks, pollution at uranium mines and the catastrophic results of failures like Chernobyl in Ukraine, (formerly in U.S.S.R.), Windscale in Britain, Three Mile Island in the U.S.A, and more recently; the tragedy of Fukushima in Japan.

At about the same time, we were also being assured by the positive thinking academics, the experts of how automation and computer development would become the wonders of the New Age, giving us more leisure time and an elevation in our standard of living.

A positive deception.

Fifty years on, we have seen how these wonders have given us more leisure time ... people have been put out of work! Computers have increased our standard of living by encouraging us to live beyond our means with the use of credit cards. We are all now deeper in debt than ever to banks and other usurers. Meanwhile, those who were able to resist the social pressures and temptation of living on credit, i.e. maintaining a negative attitude toward 'progress', are the ones who now have an advantage ... they have cashing.

We used to be a nation of savers. We used to save up for something we wanted. Now we have become a nation of borrowers. If all our creditors called in their debts, we would be left naked and living in caves, in the style of our Stone Age ancestors.

Consider the predominant characteristics of the typical trendy, vocal, team-inspiring positive thinker: selfish, conceited, arrogant, ruthless, greedy and shallow; unable to be a successful person without the efforts and sacrifices of others. Does this not describe the main body of the people who are responsible for most of the troubles that have turned the world upside down throughout history?

The history of mankind is littered with the wreckage and great tragedies caused by positive thinkers who have convinced themselves of their infallibility and inevitably brought disaster on others; as well as themselves. One of the earliest examples is recorded in the Bible; Genesis 11.1.9. Wherein the descendants of Noah, in the ancient city of Babylon, convinced themselves with their PT, that they could construct a tower high enough to reach all the way to heaven. For their arrogance and presumption, God made their speech incomprehensible to one another, with the result that the unfinished tower collapsed and the people were scattered.

Most people have heard of Napoleon 1st. History records that this pint-sized positive thinker was responsible for the needless deaths of thousands. After emerging with his commission from the French Military School in 1785, he achieved enough success in his campaign against the Austrian forces to the point where his inflated ego had him convinced by 1798, that he could crush the British Empire.

His French Fleet took on the British, commanded by Admiral Horatio Nelson, at Aboukir Bay in Egypt, and was effectively destroyed. Still undeterred, with his PT in full flight, Napoleon was convinced that anyone else was to blame but him. He joined a conspiracy to overthrow the French Directorate, the governing body at the time and appointed himself as First Consul. Matters at home kept him occupied for a time, but, ever the positive thinker, he was soon warring with his neighbours again and by 1803 he was busy assembling a huge invasion fleet for a direct assault on England. He failed, however, to take into account that greater forces than he existed, and his fleet was wrecked repeatedly by savage storms, without ever leaving port.

Ever the positive thinker, he switched his aggressive intentions to his neighbours on the European continent, until in 1805, he had another crack at the British fleet and, you guessed it ... was severely trounced again—at the Battle of Trafalgar.

Apparently by this time, he had become fed up with the fighting capabilities of the French Navy and decided to switch his confidence back to the Army. By 1812, he had assembled his 'Grand Armee' of 500,600 men and decided to invade Russia. His PT would not allow him to take seriously the enormous logistic problems that went with taking a huge army so far from home into hostile country. Nor did he allow for the approaching Russian Winter, or the determined resistance he would encounter from the Russian civilian population. They burned the grain crops to deny food supplies to the invading army while the Czar's smaller groups of cavalry continually harassed and destroyed Napoleon's supply lines and whittled away his weakened stragglers.

By the time Napoleon reached Moscow, having suffered heavy losses along the way, the cruel Russian Winter had set in and he was confronted with the additional problem of finding adequate shelter, as the city had been set on fire and many of its buildings destroyed.

Forced to retreat, (he would have called it a tactical withdrawal), he finally made it back to Paris with his ragged, starving and demoralised 'Grand Armée' reduced to one fifth of its original number of men. His neighbouring enemies Austria, Sweden, England, and, of course, Russia, seized the opportunity to unite and attack, invading Paris in 1814.

You would think that by this time, his repeated defeats and the responsibility of causing the deaths and suffering from countless thousands would have weighed heavily on Napoleon's conscience. He was mercifully exiled to Elba, where he should have spent his time writing his memoirs, but instead, he spent it plotting his escape, and amazingly, gathering renewed support from his faithful followers to raise another army. He and his army were consequently thrashed at the Battle of Waterloo in 1815. Napoleon was again exiled, this time to St. Helena, where this time his P.T. could not save him from succumbing to a terminal cancer, six years later.

As a positive thinker, he was a major player. As an aggressive, egotistical squanderer of human life and resources, his positive attitude was a monument to futility, causing wholesale misery and destruction.

Less than half a century later, the American Civil War became another tragic example of P.T. gone completely out of control. Historians do not agree about its basic causes, but it has been judged as being criminally stupid and unnecessarily bloody, brought about by arrogant extremists i.e. positive thinkers and blundering politicians. (Is there any other kind?!)

A product of this national tragedy was a bright young positive thinker named George Armstrong Custer. The youngest General in the Union Army, he achieved distinction in such notable battles as Bull Run and Gettysburg. His positive attitude received official recognition, and at the end of the conflict, he was assigned to the 7th Cavalry with the rank of Lieutenant Colonel.

He set about using his energies to massacre as many of the indigenous Indian population as possible, and in particular, to annihilate the Sioux Nation. During the course of this, while under the command of General Terry, Custer's regiment of 600 men was on a reconnaissance mission to locate the Indian encampment and assess its strength. They came upon the enemy camp at Little Big Horn, Montana, and Custer, ever the positive thinker, decided not to wait for the arrival of Terry s main force, but to attack at once and thus make a name for himself. He divided his regiment into three parts, sending two of them to attack further upstream, while he himself, led the third, numbering over 200 men in a direct charge.

Alas, his P.T. did not contemplate the possibility that his enemy had laid a cunning trap, and they, with overwhelming numerical superiority, lay concealed in ravines. The result was the complete slaughter of Custer and the men who he had led into the direct assault. The remaining force who he had deployed up-stream found themselves in deep trouble also and were too occupied with their own problems to be of any assistance in preventing the carnage that Custer had led his men into.

Custer's spectacular death, along with his 200 unfortunate soldiers, made him a popular but controversial hero—another typical example of a positive thinker who thought himself ten feet high and bullet-proof.

In more recent times, one of History's most memorable and infamous positive thinkers would have to be Adolf Hitler. Born in 1889 the son of an Austrian customs official, young Adolf lived the life of a typical 'hippy' until he joined the Bavarian Army at the outbreak of World War One. His experience in the war hardened his extreme nationalism and his hatred of Jews and Bolsheviks. After the war, he became a formidable figure in German politics as leader of the National Socialist German Workers Party.

While serving some time in prison, after an unsuccessful attempt to seize control of Germany's government, he wrote 'Mein Kampf' with the aid of a fellow prisoner, Rudolf Hess. Filled with anti-Semitic outpourings, it also extolled his worship of power, contempt for morality, and his strategy for world domination.

The Great Depression brought his Nazi Party mass support. His magnetic oratory of hate and power, his insight into mass psychology and his mastery of deceitful strategy resulted in his rapid rise to power and the backing of German bankers and industrialists. In 1934, he became the Fuhrer of the Third Reich and embarked on a large-scale rearmament programme. By 1939 he had commenced his first steps towards world domination by invading Czechoslovakia, then Poland, resulting in the beginning of World War Two.

By 1941, he and his Nazi followers believed they were invincible. So obsessed were they with their P.T. that they broke their treaty with Stalin and invaded Russia. At the infamous Battle of Stalingrad, Hitler's forces suffered huge losses of men and equipment, but 'Der Fuhrer' refused to admit defeat. He had apparently learned nothing from the bitter experience suffered by Napoleon a century before, and like Napoleon, his P.T. resulted in disaster.

Hitler's repeated strategic blunders and his obstinate refusal to listen to advice from his more capable generals had put Germany in a hopeless situation by 1945, yet he insisted that they must fight to the death. On April 30th that year, he reportedly took his life when the Russians entered Berlin. Hitler's positive attitude left as its monument, the devastation of the Nation he ruled, and a legacy of one of the most destructive tyrannies of modern times.

Of course the gurus of P.T. would be quick to dissociate themselves from the aforementioned, rather preferring that they not be remembered. They would hasten to draw our attention to the other individuals, who, by their sheer courage and indomitable spirit, overcame their personal tragedy, disability, or financial setback. Such people do indeed deserve full credit, but to attribute their triumph solely to positive thinking, they are ignoring the other qualities which were the MAIN factors resulting in their ability to overcome their misfortunes. These heroes, who by their sheer courage and determination, overcame seemingly insurmountable odds, did not expect others to support them, make sacrifices for them, or take risks for them. They made it on their own, not giving in nor looking for others to blame for their failures or set-backs along the way.

To my way of thinking, these brave souls are not your seminar conductors, lecturers, motivators or false prophets; they are the individuals who have the REAL qualities that we broadly refer to as 'GUTS'.

There is probably no one more irritating than the banal, self-opinionated ass who announces, "There is no such thing as luck; I believe in Positive Attitude" or other nonsensical statements with a similar meaning. The truth of the matter is that these types are so blinded by their own egotism that they fail to see how good fortune, fate or circumstances have guided and protected them at crucial times in their lives. When appraising the misfortune of someone we know, who has fallen on hard times, a more intelligent remark would be, "There, but for the grace of God, go I."

Most of us with enough intelligence and perception to observe the realities of life, as we progress through it, can easily recollect times in our lives or in the lives of others, where luck, either good or bad, has simply happened in circumstances beyond the control of the recipient. There are those who seem blessed with continual good fortune. There are others who, try as they might, never seem to get a fair share of it. The former are the ones who like to profess themselves as positive thinkers. They tend to be arrogant, conceited and totally lacking in compassion for the latter, who they pass off as 'losers', which makes their arrogance even more contemptible.

Positive thinkers too often give themselves all the credit for their good fortune, are crashing bores to listen to and in all probability, drink their own bath water. The positive thinkers who refuse to face reality, reject the qualified opinions which are contrary to their own and who ultimately take others down with them, but never take the blame, are a positive menace!

Unfortunately, many of today's corporate bosses and their aspiring, obsequious subordinates fit easily into this category. Driven by an underlying desire to impress the world, they unwittingly reveal their own basic insecurity and inherent dislike or dissatisfaction with themselves. Secretly aware of their own inadequacy, they incessantly harangue, lecture, preach and invoke the virtues of PT to their captive audiences and in doing so, hope to use the efforts of their minions and followers as rungs or steps on which they expect to ascend the ladder of success and achievement—a goal they could not otherwise attain, if left to their own limited capabilities.

Positive thinkers are all too frequently out of touch with reality. Any realist who contradicts or questions their judgement is branded as a negative thinker. Metaphorically, a realist might say, "Keep away from the edge of the cliff, or you might fall." The positive thinker would reply, "There is no cliff. You are a negative thinker." Again, the realist might say, "Driving through a red light is inviting disaster." The positive thinker would retort, "The lights are always green for me. You are just a negative thinker."

WELL WORN CLICHES WITH APPROPRIATE RESPONSES (with apologies to Murphy)

There are many well-worn clichés that we hear, ad-nauseum, coming from positive thinkers with monotonous regularity. Mostly short on originality, invariably irritating and insensitive, they are bandied about with the same lack of imagination that religious zealots display when continually quoting scriptures.

We should arm ourselves with suitable responses for the inevitable occasions when these boneheads start flapping their jaws. I have listed a few of the most irritating and/or offensive of these clichés with responses which I suggest would be appropriate. Keep in mind that many of these hackneyed phrases are used to spur you on, using the old principle of dangling the carrot in front of the donkey to make it move. To assume that a donkey is that stupid is bad enough. To assume that we humans are all as stupid as donkeys is a positive insult.

1.   WHEN THE GOING GETS TOUGH, THE TOUGH GET GOING.

R; When the going gets tough a life of crime looks more attractive. Of course what they really mean is that you, the lackeys, the subordinates, the unappreciated, are expected to go that extra mile—with them on your back! Who the hell are they to judge whether you are tough or not? Surely the fact that you are still persevering when the going gets tough, is evidence that your resilience is not lacking. Perhaps, with these types of uninspiring, unimaginative fools at the helm, it would be best if you did get going ... out the door to a more successful place of employment or a more rewarding occupation.

2. YOU ONLY GET OUT OF LIFE WHAT YOU PUT INTO IT

R; You only get out of life what you can take from others ... and hold onto it! This, of course, is a favourite platitude used by those who, in the main, have put very little into the fortunate circumstances that they have come into. Most of the people who I have heard spouting this hypocritical affront to the less fortunate, are greedy, selfish and conniving predators, who make a practice taking far more than they ever give. Try convincing those who have given their most useful and productive years to their children, raising them, nurturing them and making sacrifices for them, only to be cast aside like dirty sox when age, infirmity or poverty renders them of no further use to their selfish, callous off-spring. Or suggest that such rewards for effort, courage and a lifetime of honest labour await the pensioner, when he or she reads the papers and learns of the various rorts and other shady dealings involving our politicians, most of whom never did any real work in their entire lives.

3. HARD WORK NEVER KILLED ANYONE.

R. Hard work never killed anyone ... so long as they could delegate it to someone else.

Born from a combination of ignorance and indifference, this idiotic and manifestly incorrect statement is still uttered by modern day slave-drivers. Heart failure, stroke, deterioration of various joints in limbs and spine, and mental breakdown are just a few of the results from hard work. Hard work, without relief or respite, has, throughout history, taken the lives of countless thousands of slaves, convicts and factory workers in earlier times and it still kills people today.

4.   KEEP YOUR NOSE TO THE GRINDSTONE.

R. Keep your nose to the grindstone ... and you will lose it.

Nowadays this would be regarded as unsafe work practice. Furthermore, if you are so engrossed with your work that you never lift your head and cast your eyes about to see what is going on around you, you may become very narrow in your outlook and oblivious to what may be happening to your detriment.

5.   THESE THINGS ARE SENT TO TRY US

R. These things are sent to try us ... for what? Here is one of the most vacuous and meaningless placations used by the more fortunate when they don't want to be bothered offering any assistance to someone less fortunate than themselves. What they really mean is, they couldn't care less. Logically, when anyone or anything is put to a test, it is for a specific purpose. I have yet to hear an intelligent explanation of the specific purpose for which many unfortunates are the victims of all kinds of torment, abuse and degradation which seem to be unjustly inflicted upon them. Many go to their graves, none the wiser as to what their misery was testing them for, since no earthly purpose ever presented itself during their entire miserable lives.

6. THERE IS ALWAYS SOMEONE WORSE OFF THAN YOURSELF.

R. There is always someone worse off than yourself … and a hell of a lot who are better off, and a damn sight less deserving too! This banal platitude is another favourite remark used by the indifferent. True though it may be, (and we can only feel that the poor coot at the end of the line must be in a terrible state), it fails, none the less, to solve anyone's problem. Try using it with the bank when you can't keep up with your mortgage payments! I doubt that it will invoke any sympathy. Has such a crass utterance ever helped a blind person to see, or raised a cripple from the wheel-chair? It is no less stupid than saying 'Things could always be worse'. Another example of stating the bleeding obvious, but of no comfort whatever.

7. MONEY ISN'T EVERYTHING.

R. Money isn't every thing … but to quote the famous Alfred E Neumann, 'It sure beats whatever comes second. More often than not, the clown who bleats this obtuse platitude, is quite financially secure, but has no intention of giving any away. It is common to hear the old follow-up: 'So long as you have your health'; uttered in the same breath. Again, I would like to remind those bone-heads that it will cut no ice with the bank, or the landlord, and certainly not with the taxation office. You may indeed be initially blessed with robust health, but without the necessary where-withal to cushion the rough journey through life, you will be missing out on an awful lot. Many poor souls have started out with good health, only to lose it through the continual stress of trying to succeed, or even just to survive, in a world where it takes MONEY to raise your quality of life above that of a stray dog.

8.   THERE IS ALWAYS A LIGHT AT THE END OF THE TUNNEL.

R. There is always a light at the end of the tunnel ... but it may be an express train about to run you over. When you find yourself stumbling in the dark, tread very carefully and take nothing for granted.

9.   IF AT FIRST YOU DON'T SUCCEED, TRY AGAIN.

R. If at first you don't succeed, try again ... then stop before you make a fool of yourself. There is, after all, such a thing as beating your head against a brick wall. Save yourself a lot of unnecessary grief and look for an alternative or a compromise, while you are still able. Life is not a walk in the park; it's more like being lost in the jungle.

10. PUT YOUR BEST FOOT FORWARD.

R. Put your best foot forward ... and use it to kick a positive thinker. They all deserve a good kick. Give me a realist, any day. He will be far less likely to get you into trouble.

In the past, I attended many seminars and lectures, all of which, through positive thinking, were supposed to turn us all into super sales people, primed and ready to unleash our zeal on a gullible world, and make our fortunes. In due course, it became apparent that the lecturers were all vulnerable to contradiction. Some of them, in fact, became quite irate when confronted with a question or remark that challenged their doctrine. They simply had no answer. They realised that their credibility was under threat, with no intelligent defence. They then resorted to personal ridicule in a transparent attempt to embarrass the offender into silence. Apparently, when attending a P.T. seminar, the rule is you must never question what the great guru tells you, even when it is obviously rubbish.

It does require a certain amount of moral courage to be an outspoken 'negative thinker' or realist. Having an opinion contrary to that which is commonly accepted, or considered as fashionable or contemporary, immediately exposes one to being superciliously branded as a negative thinker. Such individuals are not daunted by the prospect of being made the object of ridicule by the proponents of established mores and dogmas, when these are questioned or challenged. Nor do they retreat from the jeers and criticisms that are directed at them by the brain-washed and brain-dead conformists, who blindly and obediently accept the dictates of the 'experts'.

Some of the greatest visionaries, and noted and revered achievers, have undoubtedly been the objects of derision by their contemporaries and been branded as negative thinkers or heretics. Such a man was Galileo Galilei. Born in 1564, Galileo became a great mathematician and trailblazer in astronomy. He did not accept the popular doctrine at the time, that earth was the centre of the universe, as taught by the Church of Rome. Instead, he supported the Copernican belief that the sun was, in fact, the centre of a great system, with earth being one of its orbiting planets. For this blatant contradiction and negative attitude he was denounced as 'dangerous to faith' and eventually tried by the inquisition, then imprisoned.

Charles Robert Darwin bravely flew in the face of accepted religious teaching, when, in 1859, he published his well researched theory 'Origin of Species'. The basis of his belief, still vehemently contested by religious fundamentalists, was that all life evolved from a common ancestral origin. Had he been alive to promote those views during the time of Galileo, he probably would have suffered a much harsher punishment than Galileo did. It is apparent that while today's churches have reluctantly come to accept irrefutable evidence that Copernicus and Galileo were correct after all, there are many who obstinately refuse to associate evolution with God, even though all scientific evidence indicates that our creator did not simply pick up a man and dump him on the planet in his present-day form. Surely, that is like claiming that the first aircraft to be invented was the Boeing 747 .

Johnathan Swift, the author of the classic masterpiece *Gulliver's Travels* would, by contemporary followers of P.T., be branded a negative thinker. Always the rebel, Swift was the author of various other works such as *Tale of a Tub*, a satire on religious excesses, and, as in Gulliver's Travels, demonstrated his scorn for the absurd pride of the human animal, exposing the various ways that man contravened and sinned against the laws of nature. In that regard, unfortunately, nothing has changed in the subsequent two hundred and fifty years since the book was written.

How many of his contemporaries must have called Winston Churchill a negative thinker. It was during his time as a backbencher in the British House of Commons, during the ten years prior to the outbreak of World War Two, that he repeatedly issued warnings of the Nazi threat, which went unheeded. Later, in 1946, while on a visit to the United States, he warned America of the threat posed by the U.S.S.R. to world peace. He opposed the expansion of colonial self government. Fifty years later, how many of Britain's former colonies can boast a success in self government: consider the tragedy of human suffering, genocide, corruption and economic disaster that has followed self-government of former colonies in Africa, as one example. Unlike most politicians, Churchill knew what he was talking about, most of the time. Most negative thinkers do, because they are realists.

How many times do we hear of people in business going bankrupt, or suffering severe financial loss, through making bad decisions. These disasters are not restricted to the small businesses, like the little shop on the corner. They also happen to large corporations and the multi-nationals. If we were to analyse each individual case, it would conclusively illustrate that nearly every one of them could have been avoided, or at least mitigated by a more negative i.e. cautious, or realistic, even pessimistic attitude before the bad decisions were made.

Recent times have shown how large financial institutions have lent excessive amounts to high profile entrepreneurs who flew too high, and like the legendary Icarus, crashed. A more negative attitude on the part of the lenders and investors would have avoided the subsequent losses to all concerned.

Then there are the individuals who, blinded with positive attitude, venture into their own businesses with optimism and enthusiasm only to have their finances demolished and their hearts and minds broken when unforeseen events undermine their best endeavours. Afterwards, there is plenty of time for post-mortems and hind-sight, which ultimately illustrates how a more negative attitude might have saved them from making that first bad decision. 'We should have etc.' or 'We shouldn't have' are the words so often uttered later on, in typical hindsight, both of which could be paraphrased by saying 'If only we'd been more negative, we wouldn't have.'

Predictably, my critics, professed positive thinkers, will be quick to make such comments as 'Without positive thinkers, there would be no progress', or 'If we'd listened to negative thinkers, there would be no aeroplanes, no cars, no advances in medicine or science, and we would still be living in the Dark Ages'. To them I say, we should not confuse realists with the class of those belonging to The Establishment.

Throughout history, it has been The Establishment who have hindered and delayed progress. By The Establishment, I mean those established, influential people who have created a comfortable niche for themselves, by using and perpetuating accepted doctrines and beliefs of their time. They resist new thoughts and hypotheses, because they simply dread the prospect of being proven wrong, or having their reputations and influence placed in jeopardy. They are the real negative thinkers.

It was The Establishment who persecuted Galileo and who would have called him negative, had the term been invented then, because he challenged their accepted doctrines.

It was The Establishment who denigrated Charles Darwin, because he attempted to determine a realistic explanation for the origin of all life on our planet. Instead of accepting their dogmas and their allegories, which contained too many un-answered questions for his enquiring mind, and treated the Earth's creation like a child's bed-time story, Darwin sought to discover the truth. This was not negativism, this was realism. Darwin was not an atheist. He studied at Cambridge for the Ministry, and while he did not consider his research as challenging to the existence of a Creator, he obviously challenged the reality and accuracy of established religious dogma.

It was The Establishment that Johnathan Swift satirised in his books. He was realistic with his observations of human folly and vanity. These weaknesses are still manifestly existent and are profuse among those who align themselves with established doctrines.

It was The Establishment who refused to listen to Winston Churchill's warnings about the Nazi threat because it was embarrassing to question Hitler's motives and ambitions at a time when Britain was still recovering from the horrors and losses of World War One. Like the Ostrich, Britain's leaders preferred to bury their heads in the sand, and hope that the Nazi threat would go away. Churchill would have been accused of being a negative thinker, damaging to international relations and a trouble maker.

One of our modern realists and a true visionary is Erich Von Daniken. In his book 'Chariots of the Gods,' he challenged the established hypotheses of archaeologists and theologians and encouraged readers to consider the available evidence, and real possibility of intelligent life existing on other worlds. Of course he was attacked from all sides by The Establishment, and his suggestions, regardless of their feasibility and logic, were ridiculed. Various aspersions were cast upon him personally, for daring to challenge established theories and dogmas that have held back and discouraged attempts to discover the truth. To quote his words, 'Anyone who really seeks the truth cannot ignore new and bold and as yet unproved points of view, simply because they do not fit into his scheme of thought or belief.'

Space exploration, often maligned by humanists, and some religious organisations as a waste of money, must not be dominated by positive thinkers, or it most likely will become a bottomless pit, into which billions of dollars disappear without apparent result or benefit. Charitable (?) organisations will seize the opportunity to condemn this waste, claiming that the money could have been better directed towards eliminating poverty and disease, thereby making the world a better place for all mankind. A fine idea ... but would it?

With the resultant increase in population, where are all the people going to live? Already there are many countries which cannot adequately provide for their populations, resulting in disease, wars and starvation. Charitable? Organisations and more affluent nations throw millions at them, but the situation never improves, because hardly any of the money reaches the needy, being intercepted by myriads of administrators, opportunists and corrupt governments. Birth control would go a long way towards reducing the problem in these countries, but for many reasons, religious dogmas among them, these people are the instruments of their own destruction.

Until the people in these Third World Countries learn to address the problems of their own making, throwing money at them will not make a scrap of difference, and only serve to make millionaires out of the few who are at the head of the line. Space exploration is about much more than putting Man on Mars. It is about the survival of the very planet on which we live because of the real danger that exists of a major catastrophe occurring if the earth is hit by a large asteroid. Scientists have now concluded that the 130 million year duration of the Age of the Dinosaurs was brought to rapid extinction by just such a collision, around 60 million years ago. If we are to prevent a repeat of this horrifying possibility, we need to have the means to intercept the monster far out in space, and deflect or destroy it before it comes near the earth's gravitational pull. Therefore, the Space Programme is not the domain of positive thinkers, rather than the responsibility of realists. Only when Man has developed the technology to effectively counter the threat of meeting the same fate as the Dinosaurs, should we think about exploring for other possible worlds for human habitation. In Australia, we are facing another more immediate problem, brought about, once again, by positive thinkers. They are telling us that we can take an increase of millions in our population. Not just one or two million, but ten to twenty million, and they aren't being very selective about where they come from. Moreover, they don't ever explain where these migrants, legal and illegal, are going to live, how they are going to survive, or how our limited resources are going to cope. Our coastal cities are already beginning to burst at the seams while our regional population areas are steadily shrinking due to lack of employment, lack of amenities, and lack of interest from State and Federal Governments. Revenue from farming and grazing has been reduced by our Federal Government's 'level playing field' policy on trade, to the degree where people are walking off their properties, which in many cases, have been worked by their family for generations. This means we will have to be importing more and more food items to replace what we used to produce here.

The same applies to our manufacturing industries, already severely depleted by movement to off-shore establishments, where lower wages allow them to compete with cheaper, mostly inferior imports, from countries employing sweat-shop labour.

Since the majority of Australia's inland is a virtual or actual desert, for about 80 years out of every 100, it is realistic to say that the future centres of population will not be created or maintained in these areas without some radical changes to the climate and their accessibility. Are we really expected to believe that the migrants we are going to get will be sturdy, hard working pioneer stock? Will they be prepared to go out and battle the elements, turning our millions of acres of wasteland into a fertile Garden of Eden? Present indications are that the age of pioneers is long gone, with most of our intake preferring to be denizens of ghettos, within our city precincts, serving and expanding the tentacles of organised crime.

Australia's successive Federal Governments, over a period of decades, have been guilty of criminal neglect for allowing all sorts of undesirables and rejects from their own countries to enter and remain here, under the guise of migrants or refugees. Regardless of what part of the world they come from, East or West, the prevailing attitude of this section of migrants has been one of contempt for our laws and customs, being bent on opportunism, criminal expansion, and ultimate domination.

There is little evidence to suggest that a significant proportion of contemporary immigrants are here to integrate, assimilate or assist in the development and progress of their adopted homeland.

Certainly Australia needs to populate, but are we getting the sort of migrants who want to contribute and integrate, or do they intend to make *us* assimilate to their ways and customs? We can certainly do well without the tribal and religious hatreds that exist in other parts of the world and we already have more than enough criminals of our own! This view, despite being denounced by 'do-gooders' and others with a more serious and subversive agenda, is never the less held by many who are genuinely concerned for Australia's future in the 21st Century and is not restricted to those who are citizens by birth. Many other people who came from strife-torn countries to make a new start and who are appreciative of the significantly better lifestyle and opportunities offered for their families are equally concerned.

Negativist? Racist? NO! Although this is the well-worn tactic of denigration used by the undesirable elements who see such well-founded concern for our nation's future as a threat to their intentions. If Australia is to remain comparatively free of internal strife and retain a democratically elected government, albeit questionable in many respects, we have to adopt a realistic approach and not allow ourselves to be dictated to by interlopers. Many of these interlopers are obvious hypocrites who have the brazen hide to call us racists, coming from countries where the freedom of speech which they take full advantage of here, would not be tolerated and where there is open hostility, even armed conflict between people of the same racial background! In many of these Countries, foreigners are blatantly discriminated against, or even persecuted for failure to observe their laws and customs. Who are THEY to call anyone in this country a racist?

Taking an overall view of the problems created for us by so-called 'positive thinkers', it becomes apparent that one section of our society in particular, who profess themselves to belong to that category, has done more to undermine our established and respected standards of morality, law and order and systematically destroy the fabric of National Pride. They come under the broad classification of 'DO-GOODERS'.

It is the 'do-gooders', which include the chardonnay sipping pseudo-intellectual posers and a class of woolly-headed, out of touch buffoons who like to be quoted as 'academics', who have been the most vocal, the most nauseatingly unctuous proponents for 'tolerance' and understanding towards drug abusers, violent criminals and imported recalcitrants, while the damaging effect on their victims is unconscionably ignored!

We can blame the 'do-gooders' for the presently lamentable state of affairs where law-abiding citizens now live behind security screens and bars, their homes converted to little fortresses while the criminals walk free in the streets and parks. We can blame the 'do-gooders' for all the excuses made in the defence of violent criminals and repeat offenders when they receive soft sentences from the courts. "Diminished Responsibility" is repeatedly proffered as an excuse for various acts of brutality, vandalism, rape and child abuse. Also popular as a defence is "child of a broken home" or "victim of abuse when a child" and "now receiving psychiatric care". In cold reality, there is only ONE indefensible reason for the majority of these anti-social crimes and that is, "does not expect to suffer the consequences of his/her actions." Meanwhile, through all this wringing of hands and compassion for the perpetrators, the plight of the victims is rarely considered. It's almost as if we are expected to blame the victim for being in the wrong place at the wrong time. The traumas, pain and suffering, the long term physical and mental damage, along with the suffering experienced by the families of the victims, are apparently of no concern whatever to the Do-gooders.

We can blame the Do-gooders for the omnipresent problem of un-abated drug abuse. What incentive for abstinence to the morally weak, wet string character of drug abusers are 'shooting galleries'? If these addicts are so hell-bent on self destruction, what deterrent is presented by needle exchange centres and rehabilitation centres? The Do-gooders, far from discouraging drug abuse, are aiding the continuance and proliferation of this insidious habit.

We can blame the 'Do-gooders' and our idiot politicians for the same set of laws that prevent a law-abiding resident from taking effective action to combat an intruder, even when the intruder may be armed and dangerous, while allowing the intruder the right to sue.

We can blame the 'Do-gooders' for the ever increasing rate of car thefts and vandalism, break and enters and street crime, because the offenders, particularly the juveniles, are fully aware of the soft treatment they will receive from the court, even if they are apprehended.

What sort of insanity sanctions laws that can have a convicted child killer or rapist released, or unleashed, amongst the community after serving less than ten years in prison, while a bank robber is sent away for 15 or 20 years: If you think that the bank robber is a greater menace, ask yourself which of the two would you prefer to have living next door to you and your family.

The trouble with 'Do-gooders' and their ilk is that they are conveniently remote from the event. They have not been victims. The Christian ethic of turning the other cheek to give the offender another go at doing the same thing is hardly likely to have a beneficial result, even in the unlikely event that he has a similar Christian background. My experience and many observations concerning offenders, has shown that they regard forgiveness and compassion as a weakness to be fully exploited. All the preaching and Scripture quoting falls on deaf ears where the vicious, anti-social misfit is concerned, who, like a jungle predator, sees the weak as nothing more than a part of the food chain.

As the famous comedian and author, Spike Milligan once wrote, 'If Albert Einstein stood for a thousand years in front of fifty monkeys, explaining the Theory of Relativity, at the end, they'd still be just monkeys.'

TRENDS

At this time, the beginning of the 21st. Century, TRENDS seem to govern the behaviour, even the lives, of the majority of people in our more affluent, developed countries. We should be more negative about these insidious impositions on our dignity, our pride and our intelligence, which contribute NOTHING positive or constructive to our society or human advancement. These aberrations, for that, is what they are, almost without exception, are a manifestation of mass acquiescence to the behaviour of those minority misfits who basically crave for attention. If the general populace were not essentially a majority of mindless followers, unwilling or unable to use their intelligence, or think as intelligent individuals, these glaring examples of human folly would receive the contempt that they deserve, along with their proponents.

Sadly, the single word which collectively describes all of the current trends is UGLY. Every single trend which is in vogue, emphasises or embraces ugliness. Think about it. Look around and take note of the way people dress, the shapes of the motor vehicles that are 'trendy', the roof lines of modern buildings and their facades, the standard of television sit-coms and other popular programmes; even some of the characters and participants, in the way they present themselves. It appears that UGLY is in.

For example, many 'trendies' or fashion followers would not necessarily like, or even feel comfortable in what it is fashionable to wear. They will bear the discomfort of shoes which are completely incompatible with the shape of the human foot. The sloppier the clothes, the more ridiculous the appearance, the more 'trendy' you are. Men wear long, baggy, shapeless things, ludicrously referred to as 'shorts', which far from deserving the title, hang almost to their ankles! 'Trendy' males wear their shirts rumpled and un-ironed. 'Trendy' males shave their faces only once a week, but oddly, prefer to pay more attention to shaving all the hair from their heads! This, of course, does not apply to those whose immaturity denies them of facial hair, who instead clog up their cranial hair with goo and garish colours, sticking out in all directions and giving them the appearance of some exotic cactus. Their shirts, if they wear any, are usually filthy and have the sleeves torn off.

'Trendy' females abhor any form of attire which may enhance their appearance. The skinny ones wear shapeless, loosely hanging or belly-exposing rags, while the fat ones prefer to be seen in thin, tight-fitting pants that accentuate their obese posteriors. Black, a colour traditionally worn at funerals, and serving to indicate a depressed state of mind, is currently the 'trendy' colour for evening wear for both sexes. It is also the 'trendy' colour for day wear in cold climates; as if the wintery vista and cold, wind-swept streets were not depressing enough, we can see groups of females, all wearing long, black dresses and coats, with matching hats and shoes, giving them the appearance of a coven of witches or a murder of crows!

In addition to ugly clothing, it is also considered 'trendy' to have an ugly face and an ugly body. Those who were blessed with finely shaped features, feel compelled to disfigure their faces with studs, rings and tattoos. Females elect to cut their hair short in order to make them indistinguishable from their male counterparts. It is also 'trendy' for them to disfigure their bodies with tattoos, more studs and other ostentatious adornments, sometimes in unmentionable places, making the women of the most isolated and uncivilised tribes in Africa or South America appear conservative by comparison. While we should not scorn or denigrate these indigenous people who, due to their isolation and tribal customs, do not know any other way to dress, the females of our society have no such excuse. They choose to disfigure themselves because they are moronic in their obsession to conform with the 'trend'.

By the same reasoning, the males who choose to disfigure themselves in a like manner deserve equal contempt and derision. Earrings, bracelets and perfumes, in less decadent/liberated times, were reserved for female adornment, with exception of course, to those members of the male gender, who were not sure of their sexuality and desired to advertise their confused state of mind.

UGLY is also the 'trend' in motor vehicle styles. Those of us who can remember the cars of the 1950s and 1960s recall with nostalgia, how sleek and individually stylish they all were. Certainly it could be said that they were big and thirsty, but they all had a singular style and class about them; you could tell from a distance, a Chevy from a Ford, a Pontiac from a Buick, while the impressive avant-garde style of the Studebaker led the field, turning heads and gaining admiration from even the most conservative observers. These days, all sedans, with few exceptions, have a boringly stereotyped appearance, devoid of any sort of individuality. Lacking in style or imagination, they are to all intents and purposes, unidentifiable from one another until close proximity allows us to read the maker's name.

This is progress? Fuel economy is the motivation, according to one lame excuse I was told by a dealer. If this was even half way true, how can they explain or justify the proliferation of 'trendy' 4-wheel drive vehicles that we see on the streets and highways or parked ostentatiously on suburban driveways for passing neighbours to notice? These ugly, box-shaped monstrosities are the worst fuel guzzlers of all! As for style or individuality, they are completely devoid of either. They lead the field for ugliness; they obscure the vision of drivers behind them, or parked beside them while a majority of their owners are arrogant, ill-mannered oafs with dangerously aggressive tendencies. Originally, these vehicles were designed for rough, off the beaten track travelling. Now it seems that most of them never leave sealed roads!

Let us not overlook the apparent necessity for all 'trendies', whether they drive a sedan, a ute, or a 4x4, (the prerequisite colour for utes being blue or red), to wear that badge of micro-cephalic conformity, the familiar, inevitable baseball cap! If you suggested to them that they should display a sign on their vehicles proclaiming "CAUTION! I am a brainless, incompetent idiot." they would be incensed, yet the baseball cap conveys the same message to all those who have to share the streets and highways with them! There is no need to wear any form of head cover if your vehicle has doors and a roof! Furthermore, if you have a propensity for driving a topless vehicle, enjoying the wind and insects in your face, any dermatologist worth his fee would advise a type of head cover that protected your neck and ears, as well as your face, from the sun's harmful rays—such protection the baseball cap never provides.

Obviously, architects are also influenced by 'trends'. In the past, we have seen Mediterranean, Spanish and Ranch styles in home design come and go. When no longer in fashion, they have lost their appeal and consequently a certain amount of their value, becoming dated.

Convex roof lines are currently the trend, yet they do nothing to give any style or grace, or even aesthetic appeal to a building. My earliest memories of convex or upwardly curving roofs were the somewhat make-shift weather protection applied to back yard lavatories or dunnies. Nobody cared what they looked like, and as they were invariably and understandably placed in isolation from the house, they were ignored. Now, whenever I see a modern building with a trendy convex roof line, my reaction is to immediately identify it with a backyard dunny. Hopefully, this trend will be short-lived before irreparable damage is done to Australia's skylines.

When it comes down to reportedly popular Television programmes, UGLY is definitely in. Currently, most of the shows enjoying popularity feature ugly people. For example, one of the most highly rated family sit-coms shown on prime time every day of the week consists of crudely drawn cartoon characters, each of which are horribly ugly in appearance. Sporting and movie personalities, as well as a great percentage of contemporary pop stars, appear on camera looking like they spent the night in a storm water drain; un-kempt, unshaven and unlikeable. They present a poor example to the young and impressionable, who apparently accept them as role models. It is an indictment on our modern society when these denizens of a slob sub-culture are apparently in the vanguard of trendsetters.

When it comes to day-time television, just take notice of how many ugly people are enjoying top ratings and using other ugly people in their shows. We could be excused for wondering if there are any people left in America who know how to look or behave presentably, or even care. Certainly not everybody can be fortunate with the appearance mother nature has given them, and this is understood, but need we be confronted continually with people who are apparently proud of appearing and behaving like Neanderthal dropkicks? We should be more negative in our attitude toward these insidious impositions on our dignity, our pride and our intelligence.

We have also become victims of another trend that is probably more pervading on our daily lives than any of the aforementioned, and certainly more frustrating, more irritating and one that has been arbitrarily imposed on us regardless of our wishes.

I am referring to TRAFFIC LIGHTS. Every city and state in the civilised world employs a number of people, grouped loosely and anonymously under the title of Traffic Engineers. Ostensibly, these 'experts" are paid to mitigate the problems of congestion on streets and highways so that traffic can move with a minimum of delay, and ideally, reduce the number of collisions. Despite their tertiary qualifications and their academic status, they apparently have no intelligent or lateral thinking in their approach to surmounting the increasing problems associated with traffic control.

Their mind-set is immutably focused on traffic lights as the be-all end-all solution to everything. Nothing else by way of a solution ever seems to enter their woolly little minds. If these traffic "experts" could manage to elevate and broaden their thinking above the level of hypnotised chickens, perhaps they could comprehend the real effect that these brainless blinking robots have to the detriment of road users on whom they have been foisted, and the accidents they cause.

They have tried monitoring and controlling them with TV cameras scanning busy intersections and yet the congestion continues unabated. They have tried synchronising all the sets of lights along a busy road at each intersection; theorising that vehicles can progress unimpeded at a steady average speed of 50-60 kph, through a sequence of green lights. Again, as any frequent user of the designated road would agree, it may have looked good on paper, but in practice, it is a failure when the volume of traffic increases to peak hour level. Computers have been incorporated into their controls, in the belief that these brainless robots can work out where the greatest volume of traffic is coming from and thereby allocate more Green phases in favour of the greater number of vehicles. The congestion still occurs when intersecting or cross traffic has to be allowed to proceed and in many instances, even when there is no intersecting traffic, the robots still halt the flow on the major road, to the exasperation and frustration of the many drivers who are unaccountably delayed.

This over-use and short-sighted proliferation of traffic lights have been the indirect cause of a great many collisions with resultant injuries to people involved. An extended period of stop-start driving can try the tempers and patience of the majority of drivers, especially those who drive heavy trucks, continually having to change gears up and down, as well as braking to avoid collision with vehicles driven by impatient fools cutting in front of them! Is it any wonder then, that many drivers as a result of sheer frustration, try to beat the red light when they approach an intersection, sometimes with disastrous consequences? Again, this frustration and impatience can be carried on to manifest itself in other situations, such as excessive speed, road rage and various other risk-taking manoeuvres, all of which can end in disaster.

There are many intersections where there is no reason why traffic lights cannot be replaced by roundabouts. In roundabouts, traffic can move more smoothly, with fewer and shorter delays, when drivers are able to regulate themselves, provided they are properly educated and familiar with their approach and use. If the authorities took the initiative and embarked on an intensive education programme to make roundabouts less confusing to people, a considerable saving in time and money would ultimately be the proof of their benefit. Cost of installing a roundabout would be a fraction of the expense incurred by traffic lights. While we are living in an era of finding ways toward renewable energy and reducing the use of electricity, has any traffic engineer given a thought to the saving that roundabouts would create? They use no electricity and require minimal maintenance. As a side benefit, there are no supporting poles for motorists to accidentally collide with either! As a further thought, consider the chaos if the huge multi-lane roundabouts in London or-Paris were replaced with traffic lights!

Of course there are situations where, due to lack of foresight, the streets and intersections originally laid out by planners, or simply not planned at all, are too narrow and confined for roundabouts to be feasible. Some of the streets in Sydney for example, especially in the old inner suburbs, were never planned at all and simply had their origin as cart tracks, used by the early settlers with no thought to future growth. Now these streets are choked with traffic, day and night, and the only remedy the experts can think of is more traffic lights!

It was interesting to read an article in the February issue of a motoring magazine, back in 2004, entitled, "Rotten Roads Rile Motorists." Traffic lights were cited as the cause of despair among motorists in traffic congestion due to nearby signalised intersection problems and poor linking of traffic lights; and that was just one instance. Another complaint was TOO MANY TRAFFIC LIGHTS on such heavily used roads as Gympie Road. Another cited insufficient Green time at traffic lights. These grievances are the proof of the validity of my contention that traffic lights do NOT improve driving conditions, neither do they provide intelligent control of traffic. Worst of all, far from making any contribution to road safety, they can aggravate, frustrate and irritate to the degree where tempers and patience are pushed to breaking point. If our traffic 'experts' could only elevate their minds from the bottom of the well of un-enlightenment where they apparently reside, to see over the top, the real situation on our city roads would become obvious, and they might see more negatively about traffic lights and give more thought to roundabouts as the more sensible, more economical and ultimately safer alternative. For far too long, motorists have become accustomed to having their thinking done for them. As a result, they have become far too reliant on having signs tell them when to stop before entering a busy road or when to give way, and traffic lights telling them when to stop and when to go, instead of giving them the responsibility of thinking intelligently and logically. If these abilities were considered, encouraged or even assessed before giving them a licence, our roads would be safer and a lot less stressful.

RELIGION

The history of mankind is tragically one of wars, brutality and wanton destruction. Wars are almost invariably motivated by greed or religion or a combination of both. Always the people who suffer the most, are the ones who have the least to gain. This is historically so when wars were fought in the name of some religion. Horrible atrocities have been committed in the name of God and justified by the perpetrators as being 'The Will of God' or some other deity. Christians the world over have been assured that Christ is coming again to rule over the earth, but the question arises, what is He going to do when confronted with the daunting and enormous diversification and conflicting dogmas and doctrines that exist among the myriads of churches and cults, all of which proclaim themselves to be Christian? Many of them openly sanction discrimination, bigotry and prejudice against other faiths, even other Christian denominations. They rule their followers by intimidation and the use of brain-washing techniques that effectively destroy their ability to think logically or rationally.

Despite what my critics may say, (no doubt there will be many), I am not a heathen. I was raised to believe in God and in Jesus. When the time came for me to commence my secondary education, I was sent off to one of those 'better' schools as a boarder or resident pupil. This eminent and highly respected school was owned and operated by one of the major protestant Churches and it was there that I spent the next two hungry, miserable years in conditions similar to those of a prison.

Those pious, sanctimonious 'god fearing' Christian teachers and the ancillary staff, over that two year period taught me the true meaning of harsh discipline, abundant corporal punishment, degradation and deprivation of individual dignity. They showed me the shameless and parsimonious hypocrisy that hid behind the holy facade of the Church, the absence of compassion, the greed and inhumanity of its servants and in short, the total lack of Christianity in their thinking. It is worth noting here, that some years later, in the course of my work, I was assigned to undertake a project at Brisbane's largest prison. Over the seven weeks or so that I worked behind the walls, I was able to see for myself how hardened criminals were treated as 'guests' of Her Majesty's Prison. Let me tell you, they ate better food and more of it and enjoyed better treatment from the prison staff than we did at that 'Christian' school, while under the control of the house-masters and prefects! Today, I still feel a loathing for that school, and the church that is responsible for it. In many respects, I consider that it destroyed my incentive to complete my education to a higher level and progression to a more rewarding profession in engineering or architecture.

Many years later, during a particularly depressed and confused period in my life, I was persuaded to attend a meeting held by a group who were attached to one of the many fundamentalist Christian churches that have proliferated over recent years. I had hoped to find a church that was not rife with hypocrisy; where I could meet people and perhaps experience a friendship which was real and enduring, without the false hugs and handshakes. They seemed friendly enough in the beginning, but as time progressed and I got to know more of them as individuals and observed the way they behaved, both in and out of their meetings, a terrible truth began to dawn on me! Far from practising the teachings of Jesus, they were doing the opposite! They were covertly and unashamedly spying on one another and reporting what they found to their pastor. They squabbled, tittle-tattled and gossiped about each other in the manner of spoiled infants. At their meetings, they didn't pray to Jesus in a quiet, respectful manner; they yelled and screamed and DEMANDED that Jesus hear them, apparently convinced that He would give His attention to the one who could yell the loudest!

Their puerile behaviour at meetings, their indulgence in blatant and transparent histrionics, along with their blind acceptance of their pastor's demagogic dictates, became an anathema to me. Finally, at the last meeting I attended, a visiting pastor was pontificating to his rapt, captivated audience, when one of the flock asked, "What will happen to the world in the last days?" Perched on his stool, like some loathsome cane toad, he replied, "Personally, I can't wait for the end to happen!" So smug was his attitude, so self-righteously confident was his belief in his own salvation, regardless of the horrible destruction of this beautiful world and the enormous human suffering that would be unleashed, that he was looking forward to the event, like some child anticipating a fireworks display!

That was the end of my association with that church! Significant afterwards, was the way in which my so-called 'Christian' friends, who had frequently enjoyed the hospitality of my home and swimming pool, now chose to look straight through me in the street! My conclusion that has remained unchanged is that those Pentecostals and others who practise the same attitude under a different title, are in fact, far from being Christians and are nothing more than un-witting tools of Satan. Any cult, church or organisation that promotes bigotry and intolerance of contrary opinion, derogates other Christian faiths that are different from theirs, creates confusion in the face of established scientific evidence, piously encourages division among families and demands money in specified percentages from its followers, bears NO similarity to the example that Jesus set.

We should maintain a negative attitude towards any cult, or other organisation that employs brain-washing techniques and fear as a means of gaining control over the individual's mind and will. Any church that proclaims itself to be Christian and uses the Holy Scriptures like a battering ram ignoring reason, logic, or even truth if it suits them, and is determined to reduce anyone who questions them to a cowering, quivering wreck by threatening hell-fire and eternal damnation, deserves no credibility. Surely, this deception, fear mongering, bigotry and prejudice is the way Satan works. Satan wants to deceive us under the guise of god's teaching. Satan confuses.

Where, then, is the real truth to be found? In the Bible. Well then, in which version? Do you know that there are several in existence?

Why have holy men, in their zeal to unleash the truth upon us, seen it necessary to use different versions? We could be excused for suspecting that they had their own purposes in mind. Research reveals that celebrated extant manuscripts of the Bible are written in Greek, Latin and Hebrew. The most ancient fragments of the Hebrew text are the 2 Century B.C. Papyrus of Nash, discovered in 1902 at Fayum, in Egypt, and the Dead Sea Scrolls, containing several books and fragments of The Old Testament. The first great translation of the whole Bible was the Vulgate of St. Jerome, the Latin version still used by the Roman Catholic Church. The Greek text generally received in the East, is for The Old Testament, that of The Septuagint. The first translation of The Old Testament was the Aramaic Targum. The New Testament has come down to us in Greek. In England, there were current from early times, vernacular versions of parts of the Bible, especially of the Gospels, since the Gospel was often read at mass, in the vernacular, after the recitation in Latin.

John Wycliff was one of the first to project the publication and distribution of the Bible, in the vernacular, among the English people, and two translated versions go by his name. The next name associated with the history of the English Bible was William Tyndale, whose translation was not from Latin, like Wycliffs, but from Hebrew and Greek. Tyndale's New Testament was the first English translation to be printed in 1525-1526, closely followed by a second version by Thomas Matthew. In 1539, The Crown issued its first Bible in the name of Henry VIII and known as The Great Bible. The Geneva Bible was a revision of The Great Bible, financed and annotated by the Calvinists of Geneva. The Bishop's Bible of 1568 was a recasting of Tyndale. The King James version of 1611, made by a great committee of churchmen has had great influence and is highly regarded in English literature. The Douay version was published by Roman Catholic scholars between 1582 and 1610, later to be extensively revised by Archbishop Challoner. Apparently he didn't like what it said!

In the 19th Century, the project of revising the authorised version from the original tongues was undertaken by the Church of England. The result was the revised version of 1880-1890. Many other translations were undertaken and in the 20th Century, American scholars combined to produce—you guessed it—the revised Standard Version in 1952. New Roman Catholic translations were also undertaken—the Westminster Version in England and another complete revision of the Douay edition, sponsored by The Confraternity of Christian Doctrine in the U.S.A. was begun in 1936.

Are you confused? Just what Satan wants! Among all of these spurious interpretations and revisions, remarkably, some truth has survived, as archaeologists have discovered. Evidence of events as described in some instances seems to substantiate events mentioned in the Old Testament.

Events such as The Deluge have been described in the folklore of the American Indians, Fiji Islanders and Australian Aborigines, while the earliest known description is Sumerian, one form being found in the record of Berossas, (3rd Century B.C.) in the town of Nippur, in Iraq, engraved on a clay tablet in six columns.

The confusion of greatest concern is the multitude of interpretations, translations and revisions that have been going on for hundreds of years, to the extent that we can only guess at what was contained in the original scriptures, or what is left of them. The Gospels according to Matthew, Mark and Luke, for example, were written about 40 years after the Crucifixion. Now we are expected to accept that these old men would have still been able to accurately quote, word for word, what Jesus said, after all that time. Surely these men, who, after all, were human beings, subject to the same frailties as are present day journalists, would have been just as tempted to distort or misquote for the sake of a better story or a desired effect, safe in the knowledge that no one could challenge them after that lapse of time.

To add more confusion to all of this, Protestant and Fundamentalist doctrine tell us we must believe in the Bible, as read, and that the individual has the right to his own interpretation. The Roman Catholic Church says that the Church alone may interpret the Scriptures and that the individual may read the Bible only according to the interpretation of the Church. Why is it necessary to vary and edit the truth?

PARALLELS

Mohammed, born 570 years after Jesus Christ, considered himself, at the age of 40, to be chosen by God, as the last of the prophets and a successor to Jesus. Why? Because he had a vision that god commanded him to preach. Thereafter, throughout his life, he continued to have revelations, he claimed. Fundamentally, he taught: there is only one god and man must submit all to Him. In this world, the nations who rejected god's prophets would be punished. Heaven and hell are waiting for the present generation. The world will come to an end with a great judgement.

This all sounds very familiar, so far, to those of us who are acquainted with Christian doctrine and note the use of fear and ignorance, once again. Mohammed included as religious duties:

Frequent prayer.

Alms giving.

Usury was forbidden—in this regard, both Christians and Moslems are equally culpable.

Now how different was Mohammed from today's Christian evangelists? The Koran, the Holy Book of the Islamic faith, is supposed to contain the words of God, as they were given to Mohammed.

The Gospels according to the Saints, in our Bible, have the same basis.

The Ulema are the religious scholars who regulate religious life in Saudi Arabia.

The Pope and the Cardinals in the Vatican regulate religious life in the Roman Catholic world.

The Jima is the perceptions, or interpretations of the Koran by the religious scholars of Islam, just as Christians have been given interpretations of the Bible by Archbishops, Priests and Evangelists.

One can be forgiven then, for wondering where things went wrong between Christians and Moslems, when such similarities exist in their beliefs and methods of controlling the believers. More than likely, Moslems and Christians have been set against each other by ruthless manipulators on both sides, who use religion as a tool or instrument in order to incite mistrust and hatred between the people of both faiths to achieve their own objectives, motivated by greed for wealth and lust for power. Religion, regardless of denomination or creed, is a system of belief in, and worship of a supernatural power or god. There is no necessity to align one's self with any specific church and its own invented interpretations and dogmas. This only creates division and confusion between believers and obscures the true message of God's intention, and that is simply to believe in Him and live our lives as best we can without causing pain or harm to others. We are all His creations and as such He loves us and understands our imperfections. Certainly, we should try to correct our faults but we should never make the crass assumption of calling ourselves Saints. Neither should we be brainwashed by 'Holy Men' into fearing God as if He was some omnipresent vindictive headmaster, waiting for some excuse to punish us for any trivial transgression of the rules. He wants us to be happy in this life, but not at the expense of others. We were all given an intelligent mind so that we can make our own decisions, and not waste it by allowing other human beings, purporting to be 'Holy Men' to make decisions for us.

At this point, it is worth remembering too, that God did not invent money, and has no use for it so we should be wary of 'Holy Men" and false prophets who constantly demand money as tithes or alms in god's name. Money cannot buy God's favour. It only buys power in this world, and we are only here for a short time. God must despise all men and women who prey upon their fellows while masquerading under the guise of 'Messengers of God'. This, to Him, must be the most despicable betrayal of faith.

Do we need a church or cathedral in order to pray to God? More often than not, these man-made constructions are nothing more than an expression of vanity and an attempt to impress and show superiority in a materialistic way. Undoubtedly it impresses some people, but not God. Personally, I feel closest to God when I am surrounded, not by other people, but by the natural beauty of trees, and mountains and the expanse of open sky, and solitude. I do not need, or want groups or crowds around me, nor do I want some priest, pastor or self-styled evangelist to do my praying for me, or making out he or she has a 'Hot Line' to heaven and knows how God thinks.

Predictably, negative opinions about religion will be the object of fierce, even fanatical attack from fundamentalists and devotees of all faiths. Anyone expressing such views will be labelled with such derogatory names as Heretic, Blasphemer, Atheist or Heathen and a Danger to Faith. The undeniable truth of the matter which these name-callers will deny is that they, with their wilful and un-conscionable fragmentation of a common faith into various cults, sects, and break-away denominations, with their ensuing bigotry rivalry and conflicting ideas, have done vastly more damage to the credibility of religion than anyone else.

LIES, DAMN LIES AND STATISTICS

The reality of the times we live in is that we are told lies, practically every day of our lives. Commercialism, i.e. advertising, uses lies or exaggeration to sell a product. "Scientific tests prove" or "Independent tests show" they tell us, but nobody challenges them to be more specific. For example, who carried out the tests, if any, and what were their qualifications, and how independent were they really?

Opinion Polls allegedly conducted by the media, on all sorts of issues, some of relevance or importance, but now days becoming increasingly vacuous and irrelevant, have become practically a daily occurrence. We are assumed to be gullible enough to believe them. Take T.V. ratings, for example. How many times, if ever, have you been approached and asked to take part in a survey concerning T.V. programmes? When was the last time anyone asked you for your opinion about the Prime Minister, or the Leader of The Opposition, or the policies they expounded? More to the point, if such opinion polls were actually conducted, how impartial were they? Furthermore, who was paying for them? For instance, if you were a Pollster, being paid by a political party to conduct a poll which would produce a favourable result, you would hardly be inclined to solicit opinions in a locality where the majority of residents were sympathetic to the opposite side.

Then we have the advertisements that, while they can't be actually labelled as lies, cleverly avoid telling you the truths that await you later, when you respond to the bait. Banks are notorious for this, in the way they will impress you with a low-interest rate on a loan, but the establishment fees and other charges are conveniently over-looked in their promotion.

We are all familiar with the well-worn tactics favoured and recklessly bandied about by our politicians, and quoted as statistics. With statistics, they can tell us anything. How can we disprove them? We don't have access to the recorded information that is amassed in the cloistered perplexity that is the exclusive domain of the bureaucracy. Yet the majority of people seem to be prepared to accept statistics without question as if they could not possibly be misleading, distorted or completely false or inaccurate. Politicians attempt to justify blatant extortion with statistics. They use speed cameras and random breath tests to extort money from motorists, and when challenged use statistics as an excuse but never explain where the revenue is used, (or why it isn't,) for any good purpose. Every one can see that the enormous revenue raked in from motorists, each year, in fines, fees and excises, is not being honestly deployed on improving roads and road safety. They love to tell us how they are making our roads safer with speed cameras, when it is obvious to anyone using our roads that speed cameras are as much use to road safety as a sore back-side is to a boundary rider on horse-back(They incessantly boast about the success and effectiveness of random breath testing, but their own Police statistics, when quoted, indicate a success rate of less than three per cent at best, of the total number of drivers tested. Meanwhile, they don't explain why they 'delayed' about random testing of drivers for drug abuse, when this problem is far more wide spread and undoubtedly more lethal.

Why then, do we continue to dumbly accept these and other every-day false and misleading statements without so much as a murmur of protest or challenge? Why are we not vocally and actively negative in our response to the liars, charlatans and opportunists who rely on our diffidence, complacency and gullibility when they make nonsensical or false claims? While we continue to let them get away with it, they will continue to feed us crap with impunity.

Don't get the impression that we have our champions of Truth and Virtue in the media. They write their columns and utter their opinions on radio and TV to give us the impression that they are the forthright and un-biased voice of our social conscience, but that is all cosmetic to a large degree. In truth, they are all paid minions of powerful political and commercial interests, as past events have shown. That is not to say that they are completely facile or ineffectual. Some worthy causes have benefited from their influence, but only if the comments and opinions expressed do not offend or upset the sponsors or other benefactors.

We cannot expect to achieve any significant reform to the established prevarications committed by political and commercial interests unless we adopt a more negative attitude, en mass, to their conduct. Refuse to buy a product that uses misleading advertisements. Write to the Principals of the media that ostensibly conduct opinion polls and challenge them to prove their veracity. Change your Bank when you catch them out, making promises of attractive interest rates when there are strings attached, or when the very small print says "Conditions apply." When a Politician uses statistics to baffle us or obscure the truth, let him or her know, either verbally or in writing, that you will be voting for someone else in the next election.

SAVING LIVES AND OUR NATION WITH NEGATIVITY

Basically, we must begin by relegating the noisy minority to the background where they belong and ignoring their bleating. They are the ever vocal, attention seeking personalities among the academics and the pseudo-intellectuals and bleeding heart do-gooders who have been dictating to our politicians for too long, with the result that increasing drug abuse is continuing to destroy lives and violent criminals continue to hold our communities in terror. We have to face the fact that making excuses for criminals and drug abusers has not worked. Violent crime is on the increase and drug abuse continues to destroy lives and families, unabated. Legislating against the use and possession of firearms has achieved nothing in preventing murder and robbery. It has however, effectively disarmed the law-abiding section of our Nation, leaving them more vulnerable than before to the actions of the criminal element and seriously depleted in our defence capability in the event of foreign invasion or organised terrorist attack. Most of us who were alive here in Australia, 70 years ago, can remember how we faced the very real possibility of invasion. Our own military force was vastly out-numbered, mainly deployed overseas and it was necessary to recruit every adult male who was capable of carrying a rifle, even those graded as unfit for military service, into the Volunteer Defence Corps. Today, thanks to the short-sightedness of our politicians and the noisy minority calling themselves the 'Anti-Gun lobby' we have become deprived of the ability to become familiar with the use of firearms and severely discouraged from possessing them, even for self-defence. Predictably, those members of the Anti-Gun Lobby would be the first to howl for protection if the threat of invasion occurred again.

In the war against the enemy within our shores, i.e. the criminals, the Law has to get tough and the Judiciary must become less lenient with serious offenders. Our legislators must encourage this with harsher penalties. Anti-social crimes such as vandalism, graffiti and petty theft need to be countered more effectively and less humanely. In earlier times, before the do-gooders and their ilk were given too much attention, Police Officers were able to dispense 'rough justice' in a way that these social misfits could understand. A couple of nights in a cell or a few good, well-placed kicks did wonders in persuading them to mend their ways, thus saving the time and cost to tax payers of Court appearances when they would receive absurdly light penalties from the Judiciary anyway.

Now is the time to face reality and ask the civil libertarian do-gooders and the academic, out of touch bone-heads who support them, what has been achieved with the kid-glove treatment of anti-social misfits and violent criminals? Ask the ever vocal, attention seeking proponents of human rights, when are the rights of innocent citizens going to be considered? Why should violent criminals be allowed bail while awaiting trial when the evidence against them is conclusive? In all too many instances, they already have a record of similar, previous offences. It is disturbing to think of how many victims of these recalcitrants could have been saved, had bail been refused. One glaring example comes to mind, concerning an entire family, consisting of three young children and their parents living in Northern New South Wales in the 1980's, shot to death by a man who was out on bail after previously attempting to kill the father.

History tells us of the effective ways that justice was meted out in previous times. Minor crimes were punished by publicly shaming the villains in the market place. Hands and feet were secured in a solid wooden frame, called a Stock. Passers-by could pelt them with rotten fruit, eggs or manure. How many of us would enjoy doing that to someone who had vandalised our car or scrawled graffiti on our front fence or home or deliberately damaged a public amenity! You can bet it would deter them from committing a similar offence!

More serious crimes, excepting murder and armed robbery, resulted in a flogging. This form of punishment is still in use today in some other • Countries, not all of which can be considered backward or barbaric. How many of our modern generation would be more inclined to stay away from illegal narcotics if they knew that instead of receiving tolerance and sympathy, they would experience corporal punishment when caught. One painful experience of that would surely make a difference to their cavalier attitude, too often apparent these days. I and others of my generation can well remember how the Principals and teachers of our schools, enforced discipline with the cane. Even the most rebellious pupils were inclined to respect the rules, rather than experience the pain and humiliation that resulted if they broke them!

Inhuman! Barbaric! I can hear the do-gooders bleating. Consider which method is more likely to deter our youth from embarking on the use of narcotics; The experience of temporary pain and embarrassment and the promise of more of the same if they persist with this insidious habit? Or just slapping them on the wrist and stupidly providing them with needle exchanges, shooting galleries and facile, ineffectual preaching? We are talking about saving lives here! It is time we threw academic rhetoric into the garbage bin where it belongs and faced reality! It has not worked and it never will. The old axiom, "You have to be cruel to be kind" was never more relevant than now, when we are faced with a huge and increasing problem.

Unfortunately, the necessity for this 'barbaric' method of correction is the consequence of listening for too long to the do-gooders. If discipline was restored in the home, and in the schools, where it used to be, and where it is the most effective, we would not have the problems of today, and our Nation would be far healthier. For one instance, juvenile offenders would not be getting away with light sentences or pathetically useless lectures from a Magistrate. Juvenile crime leads to more serious offences because there is no effective deterrent handed down from the Court.

The do-gooders and smart-alec psychologists will argue against corporal punishment, but they haven't come up with any effective alternative, have they? The gaols are more over-crowded than ever and mostly out-dated, and that, of course, is another reason put forward against imprisonment for minor offenders, juvenile offenders, and some first-time offenders ... . the latter being the ones who repeatedly got away with it before being caught.

'You must not lock up these poor unfortunate misfits with vicious, hardened criminals' they tell us, and this is a plausible argument, of course. In many instances this could result in the first offender emerging from the 'correction' centre a worse criminal than before, due to the environment and influence of sociopaths, sadistic killers and recidivists, many of whom are a remorseless, callous and brutal class of predators, with no possibility of rehabilitation. They have committed pre-meditated crimes of murder, rape and torture, of the most sadistic and diabolical kind on defenceless victims. They have been and will remain a menace to society while they are alive and physically capable of repeating their vile and despicable crimes, and inevitably, under our present system, most of them are released while they are still a menace, and more human suffering is the result.

It is time we turned a negative ear to those who believe we should offer them rehabilitation, all at enormous cost to the tax payers, while they have no intention of reforming, and no genuine remorse for the suffering they have caused. By cynically taking full advantage of the system, they can reduce their confinement with the pretence of good behaviour, 'discovering God' and becoming Born Again Christians, with all the trappings of evangelism and new found love for their neighbours, but this facade is merely a means to an end. They have no genuine remorse and no intention of changing, on release, and no thought whatsoever of effectively repaying their debt to society because they hate us all, and we are all potentially part of their food chain.

It is time we demanded real protection for ourselves and our families by changing the system and re-introducing capital punishment for the perpetrators of these brutal types of crimes. We can all remember many of the inhuman atrocities they have committed, yet there they are, not only being fed, clothed and accommodated at tax payers expense, and meanwhile having the hide to lodge appeals against the length of their sentences because they have 'Rights'! How ludicrous.

The do-gooders love to come up with statistics from dubious research, often accredited to some source in the U.S.A. that claims that capital punishment is not a deterrent to violent crime. Well, the best statistic is the truth, and the irrefutable truth is that when a vicious, sadistic killer or rapist is executed, there is no longer any threat of him or her ever claiming another victim. How's that for a deterrent?

"What a waste of human life'" some will say. "There must be a way we can make these human beings contribute to the benefit of society they will preach. Well, there is ... .and after their execution!

They can significantly contribute to the benefit of the society they have so horribly offended while they were alive, by donating their healthy organs.

The perennial problem of finding organ donors would be significantly relieved and many innocent sufferers who have been waiting for months, or even years for replacements would be given a new lease of life. What better way could vicious killers atone for their crimes than by saving lives?

Forget about the "rights of monsters who have tortured, degraded, murdered and defiled their victims in the most inhuman fashion! They recognised no rights for the hapless human beings who they mercilessly vented their savagery on. They had no regard for the rights of the families left behind, who have suffered life sentences of grief and mental agony as a consequence. Why should our society continue to depend on the charity and humanitarian motives of law-abiding citizens for organ donations while the atrocities committed by our worst criminals go unatoned?

The whole system of dispensing justice is presently lame and inadequate. Law-abiding citizens are not living under the protection of the Law and we know it. Honest Police Officers know it, and so too do the criminals. What use is in a Jury handing down a guilty verdict for a violent crime, when the accused receives a ridiculously light sentence from the Magistrate? How demoralising it is for the Police Officers who see this happening all too often, after they have diligently worked and devoted inestimable hours, sometimes amounting to years, to bring these menaces to justice, only to see some Judge impose a shorter sentence than the Law provides for, and for reasons that 'His Honour' does not have to explain' From bitter experience, our Police Officers know that too many of these offenders are released after an un-justifiably short period of imprisonment, only to go out and re-offend. Thus the time and effort the Police expended in putting them out of circulation, and dis-regarded by the Magistrate, was effectively to little avail.

The obvious conclusion is that the present system must be overhauled. Magistrates must no longer be allowed to behave as if they were God, and should be answerable to the people they are supposed to serving. Who is paying their huge salaries after all? The way to remove their God-like status is to operate the Court in the same way that large Companies do, when making policy decisions. They have a Chairperson and a Board of Directors, who all meet and discuss the matter under consideration before the Chairperson calls for a vote on how the matter should be addressed. In the case of a Court of Law, the Magistrate would be the Chairperson and the members of the Jury would form the committee or Board of Directors. After hearing all of the evidence the Jury would retire with the Magistrate to consider a verdict. The Magistrate would preside, while the Jury debates and he would inform them as to the minimum and maximum sentence applicable, should a verdict of guilty be reached. Those present, should the accused be found guilty, discuss the length of sentence and vote on it. They may decide on a suspended sentence, if there are mitigating circumstances, or a more severe punishment, as they would all be fully informed on the case. In this way, the sentencing procedure would not be the sole domain of the Magistrate, while the Jury, being composed of members of the Public, would play an important role in the way that sentences are handed down. This is only fair. The Jury consists of people from various stations in life ... rich and poor; professional and business people, white collar workers and blue collar "battlers', all representative of the law-abiding citizenry to who the Law owes a duty of care. All too often it seems, Magistrates, due to their academic background and their generous salaries, along with a comfortable life-style, are sadly out of touch. How many of them ever had to get their hands dirty? How many of them have ever experienced the anxiety and hardship of being unemployed? Have any of them or their families ever been the victims of a violent crime? Do they have any idea of how it feels to be heavily in debt and on a low income?

The age of Dinosaurs is long past and so too should be the present concept of British Justice, where the status of the Judiciary was exclusive to the 'ruling class'. i.e. the wealthy aristocracy and the privileged. We like to think that we live in an egalitarian society, yet in the 21st. Century, we are subjected to a legal system where a false aristocracy has the authority to administer 'justice' while enjoying an attitude of complete detachment and obvious indifference to the consequences of their ethereal decisions.

They should not complain when the responsibility of passing sentence is shared with the members of the Jury. This would have the advantage of absolving the Magistrates from the insinuations of personal interests, bribery or intimidation that may otherwise ensue, while still maintaining their status within the system. It is, said and rightly so, that justice should not only be done, but should also be seen to be done, yet presently, in too many instances, it is not apparent in either respect.

NATIONAL SERVICE

This controversial subject will always bring it's opponents out of the woodwork with all sorts of reasons as to why it should not be re-introduced. Certainly the inexcusable decision on the part of a previous Prime Minister to commit National Servicemen to active duty in Viet Nam, did considerable harm to the concept of National Service. Australia was not under the threat of invasion, nor had we been under :a attack, yet these men were conscripted and sent to war solely for the purpose of a Prime Minister of no significance ingratiating himself to the President of a powerful Country. Since then, the thought of a similar scenario being re-enacted by another politician with ambitions for world recognition, has put the stratagem into disrepute.

Other reasons for it's unpopularity are based on expense and a lukewarm reception from the Military themselves, who have become more selective in who they are prepared to accept for training. Sadly, since the 1970s, a great many young men and women have rendered themselves completely unfit for any useful activity by becoming drug dependent, and unable to think straight, see straight or shoot straight. However, National Service need not be identified as being service in the Military, as we have been accustomed to thinking.

A visit to any Centrelink office will reveal a huge and untapped resource of labour among the 18 to 25 age group, who either cannot or will not find suitable employment. While many of them may not be classed as fit for the demands and rigours of military service, they are, none the less, fit enough to be put to some useful purpose, instead of being left to their own devices. Instead of being conscripted for military service, why shouldn't they be conscripted to serve the Nation in organised and supervised establishments, administered along the same lines as a military base, possibly by ex-military personnel. There are many worth-while and necessary projects that could be undertaken in this manner, such as labouring on farms, or collecting the huge amounts of rubbish that have been discarded along our highways by thoughtless slobs. Then, there are other problems that could be addressed, such as the salinity of formerly arable land along the Murray-Darling basin. Tree planting could be undertaken over these affected areas to restore valuable farm land. Or more ambitiously, how about constructing a pipeline to bring the stored water from Lake Argyle down to the drought- susceptible farm lands of Western Australia? Presently, much of this enormous volume of water is un-used, and each year, in the wet season, it is allowed to flow out into the Timor Sea. What a waste.

There are so many Nation - building tasks that could be under-taken in this manner, by National Service, without any need for service in the Military. There is no doubt, however, that an imposed environment of military style discipline and conduct is just what many of our young people need to restore them to a state of physical and mental health and teach them self respect. One of the many benefits of National Service was that it gave a sense of purpose to those trainees who otherwise may not have felt that they were doing anything worthwhile with their lives. It gave them a certain pride of accomplishment, taught them the importance of team-work and, probably most significantly, they experienced the bonding of mate-ship, while at the same time, realised the importance of discipline in bringing a sense of order and responsibility into their lives.

Prior to the Viet Nam experience, most 'Nashos' admitted that they had enjoyed and gained from their time in the Army, and made long-lasting friendships. Some enlisted as regulars afterwards, and achieved worth-while careers, learning useful skills and were assisted in further education.

If this proposal sounds like adopting a positive approach to the problem of youth un-employment and drug abuse, just wait for the predictable reaction from the do-gooders. Human Rights academics and Civil Libertarians will strenuously and vociferously denounce it as negative, draconian or even fascist. Apparently they are quite happy to preserve the status quo, watching our Youth destroying themselves in 'shooting galleries' living in squalor and depravity on streets and in parks and resorting to crime to finance their addictions.

MIGRATION

There is no denying that the growth and development of Australia as a Nation, in a remarkably short period of time, compared to other Nations, was due to migration. Before the First Fleet landed in 1788, this continent was a wilderness, inhabited only by nomadic indigenes who existed solely by hunting and gathering. They had none of the engineering, farming or weaponry skills possessed by the in-coming Europeans, who soon outnumbered them. Their destiny, tragically, was to suffer the same fate as the other indigenous peoples of North and South America. Inevitably, the expanding population and accompanying turmoil that existed on the European continent and the British Isles in the seventeenth, eighteenth and nineteenth centuries resulted in a desire to escape from the resultant hardships and persecution among the millions of oppressed. Others were lured by the promise of un-tapped wealth that they believed existed in the mysterious land on the other side of the world.

Australia was therefore destined for an influx of migrants and if it had not been the British, it would eventually have been the French, Russian, Dutch, Spanish, or even the Chinese who would have claimed it as their own. Under any one of these it is doubtful that the Aboriginals would have received any better treatment. Then as recently as the early 1940's Australia came very close to being invaded by the Japanese. Dissenting Aboriginals in this era who still prefer to harbour a grudge against white people, despite the money and effort spent in attempting to compensate for the sins of past generations, would do well to remember that it was mainly the white men and women who suffered and sacrificed their lives to defend Australia then. Moreover, there is no doubt that under Japanese domination, all the Aboriginals would have been swiftly exterminated or enslaved!

Admittedly the early European settlers were in many instances harsh and cruel in their treatment of Aboriginals, but if you look at their history, they were equally harsh and cruel to one another. They knew very little about compassion. Convicts were beaten, starved, raped and frequently murdered by their guards. Many did not even survive the long sea voyage from England as a result of their treatment, while the majority were convicted and deported for very petty offences, which in many instances were committed in an attempt just to survive.

Having said all that, these same people, both convicts and free men and women, were the ones who worked and contributed to the development of our Nation. They pioneered the land, exploring and opening up new territory for farming that hitherto had been un-developed and un-productive. The benefits that we all enjoy today are due to the courage, determination and perseverance of the thousands of immigrants who came here, without the expectations of an easy living, knowing full well that there would be no welfare organisations and no Government subsidy to provide for their support.

Multiculturalism is very trendy at present, and certainly, in the past, Australia has benefited, but, how things have changed over the last 50 years! It has become increasingly apparent that a great many immigrants, including those claiming refugee status, have arrived in Australia with entirely different expectations from those of their predecessors. They expect not only to be supported, accommodated and tolerated for their contempt for our laws and customs, but they show no inclination to assimilate, either.

Instead, the impression they project, is that we, their benefactors, should assimilate and acquiesce to their beliefs and traditions, while they denigrate ours.

If we leave it to the politicians, they will sell us out to whoever can offer them the most votes or material rewards and Australia will lose its identity to foreign extremists and fanatics. In their typically short sighted and contemptible approach to their responsibilities, our politicians apparently overlook the fact that their own children and grandchildren will inherit the results of their folly, along with every other Australian. Instead of dumbly ratifying their short-sighted and mercenary attitudes by accepting their policies, we need to shake off our quasi-positive 'She'll be right mate' attitude and start becoming more negative and assertive toward reminding them of their responsibilities.

A new, dare I say, more negative approach toward encouraging the right type of migrants is urgently needed. Instead of submissively doing nothing while they gravitate to their suburban ghettos, and reverting to the ways and traditions of their ethnicities, it should be made clear to them that they have an obligation to assimilate, and contribute to the Country, while they enjoy its privileges.

Firstly, they should have to pass a test for an ability to communicate in the English language. Secondly they must be prepared to accept work wherever they are needed. Thirdly, work must be made available on projects of National importance, such as highways, water conservation schemes, inland railways, improvements and extensions to city and rural water, electricity and waste disposal systems, already over-taxed in many places, where population growth is out-stripping infrastructure. Presently there are no projects similar to the Snowy River Scheme and successive governments have left the responsibility of job creation to private enterprise. If the Snowy River Scheme had been left to private enterprise, it would still be just a pipe dream.

Australia is a dry continent and is regularly affected by severe droughts, which in recent times have become more frequent and more prolonged. Why isn't the Government spending money to combat this problem? It appears that more importance is attached to boasting about a budget surplus than attending to the pressing problem of the Nation's water supply. What use is a budget surplus to the farmers who can't grow their crops, or the graziers who can't adequately feed their starving sheep or cattle, or the economic disaster suffered by the businesses in rural towns due to prolonged and frequent droughts? Then there are the coastal towns and cities which are also affected. The demand for water in these municipalities is threatening to exceed the availability of supply. It may seem to be an opportune time for various local governments to extract more money from their communities by adopting a user pay system for water supply but it does nothing to increase the supply, while the communities simply get less for their money.

Yes, there is plenty of work for all of our unemployed, not just the afore-mentioned, and a budget surplus is not achieving a damn thing to address our need to get on with real job creation where it counts.

ROAD SAFETY

It is common practice these days, for State Police Departments to have a squad of experts whose function it is to investigate and report on the circumstances associated with fatal road crashes. They interview witnesses and survivors, take photographs at the scene, and paint marks on the roadway, presumably to indicate the assumed or calculated path of the vehicle or vehicles involved, and assess the cause. The latter function we presume, is not just for determining liability, but to investigate whether road conditions may have contributed, and if so, what action the authorities should take to remedy the problem, if one exists.

It would be interesting, from a statistical and litigating point of view, to learn how many road hazards, contributing to death or injury, are created by road works.

In South East Queensland, at the time of writing, it is virtually impossible to drive anywhere without being confronted with barricades, witches hats and official vehicles with flashing lights blocking at least one half of the available roadway. Often these measures are reinforced by bored looking people holding signs, telling us when to stop or slow. Many times I have wondered whether the sign saying 'Slow' is directed at the motorist, or maybe describing the pace at which the road works are proceeding! For example, I am sure that any frequent road user can relate to instances where at least half of the road way is closed, yet nothing in the nature of road work seems to be getting done. Sometimes the only evidence of any road works is a parked truck, perhaps accompanied by an earth-moving machine, doing nothing, and parked behind the inevitable barricades, surrounded by heaps of earth and excavated road bed.

As if the frustrations and hazards of using heavily trafficked and inadequate roads was not enough, the motorist is now plagued with continuing delays and further perils as a result of road works, which in many cases could have been carried out at less busy times, should have been completed in half the time, or were perhaps completely unnecessary in the first place. Often we could wonder if some are nothing more than job creation schemes!

It is not just frustrating and irritating, but in many real instances, downright dangerous to have two or three heavily used and rapidly moving lanes of traffic suddenly reduced to one, and sometimes for the most un-necessary or un-timely purposes, like spreading top soil on the median strip, spraying weeds or filling pot-holes .... all of which could surely be done at a time when traffic is not so busy and conditions not so obviously dangerous.

Then we have more infringement on available road space at construction sites. Apparently builders and developers have special privileges that the rest of us who use the roads and footpaths do not. For them it is permissible to take up half of the road and all of the footpath with make-shift fences, heavy trucks and cranes or building materials. Double parking is also tolerated ... . for them ... and these infringements and impositions can go on for weeks, or even months. That's progress they tell us, but we are the ones who are paying for it with no ultimate benefit. If every builder or developer was levied for the use of a public footpath and space encroachment on the roadway, the funds generated could be of considerable benefit to the local Councils and, hopefully, to the rate payers. Perhaps then, these creators of chaos on our streets may become more caring in the way they go about their construction practices and less inclined towards encroaching on public space.

Road works are a perpetual anathema for road users and need to be planned and carried out intelligently, instead of operating in the present ad-hoc manner that they presently are. The safety of road users should be considered, as well as the safety of road workers. Moreover, barricades, warning signs and speed reduction signs should be removed as soon as work is completed, not left for days afterwards when they are no longer necessary. 1 END ROADWORKS' is a sign we often see after passing through these interminable man-made hazards and delays. 'I wish they would' I sometimes mutter to myself although I realise this is taking negativity too far. Surely however, it is reasonable to question the necessity of some, or the in-appropriate times when they are carried out, or more significantly, the length of time they take, considering the abundance of time and labour saving machinery that is now employed, compared to fifty years ago. Any day now, I expect to see the evidence of our mounting hostility manifested by the insertion in graffiti of the word 'ALL' on the sign, between the words END and ROADWORKS.

While on the subject of road safety, let us not leave out another major contribution to road hazards ... cyclists! All cyclists should be licensed, regardless of age. If they ride on any public footpath or road, they should be tested for their ability to ride with safety and common sense, and their awareness of the road rules. I for one, am sick of the mindless behaviour displayed by many of them, in the way they ignore fundamental rules of the road, by not stopping at red lights, not keeping to the far left hand side of the road and not displaying lights of any kind after dark. Almost anyone who drives a motor vehicle can recall instances when a thoughtless, irresponsible cyclist has almost, or actually has collided with them. It is common to see a group of cyclists riding two or three abreast along a road, taking up as much space as a car, while only moving at 10 to 20 k.p.h., For a motorist to avoid them, while overtaking, it then necessitates crossing over the centre of the road, which in many instances can result in (a) colliding with an on-coming vehicle, (b) colliding with one or more of the cyclists in an attempt to avoid incident (a) or (c) being sworn at or receiving obscene gestures from the cyclists if the driver attempts to warn of his or her approach by sounding the horn. After all, what is the horn for, if not to sound a warning to someone? Is verbal abuse and obscene gestures the way to respond intelligently to someone who is trying to warn you of imminent danger? Cyclists who are guilty of traffic violations should be subject to the same penalties as a motorist, their behaviour policed in the same manner, and they should have to be licensed, with their licences subject to the same rules of forfeiture and points loss.

Can anyone explain why these people can have free and un-limited access and enjoyment of public roads, without being asked to contribute to their maintenance and upkeep? They even have the local Councils constructing special cycle paths for them, funded of course by rate payers, while they contribute nothing towards their construction or maintenance thereafter.' while the predictable retort would be that many cyclists are rate payers, there are many more who are not. Why should a cyclist not be made to register his or her bicycle? An added benefit would be that by having to display a registration plate, any offending rider could be identified and traced in the same manner that is applied to offending motorists. Presently it is all too easy for cyclists to break the law without any fear of being penalised.

Cyclists, in attempting to justify their unwillingness to contribute anything, while the motorists and tax-payers do, like to claim that they are helping the environment by reducing pollution. If they walked, or used public transport, the same benefit would result and they would not be in the way of everybody using the road!

They also profess to be setting an example by exercising and keeping fit in this manner. This they can also achieve by walking or swimming, with a greater chance of keeping fit (and alive) by staying out of the way of motor vehicles.

Cyclists also declare that their presence on the road does no damage to the road surface; therefore this negates their obligation to contribute toward it's maintenance. The majority of motor cyclists and motor scooter owners could make the same claim, yet they not only have to register their machines, but are required to qualify and pay for a licence to ride them as well!

Another absurd statement made, is that if they own a motor vehicle, they are then already contributing their share. On the basis of that spurious argument, an owner of two cars should not have to register the second one. What rubbish!

Cyclists, especially those with enough money and spare time to indulge themselves in elaborate equipment, apparently consider that they belong to an elite and therefore are in no way associated with the proletarian masses with their tedious rules and regulations. This is one manifestation of the current 'sporting hero' syndrome, a Nationwide mind set, instigated and proliferated to a large degree by the Media, whereby Sport is akin to Godliness and those who excel in it are venerated as heroes or demigods.

Schools and colleges also promote and sanction this attitude by rewarding their sports high achievers with ego-inflating status awards such as blazers and feudal type authority over their less talented fellow pupils as a Prefect or School Captain. Qualities like leadership, sagacity and modesty are not the prerequisites for becoming a school Prefect, whereas success in dominant sports, such as Rowing, Cricket or Rugby are. These promote the School's image, it is thus: " . considered, while the rest of the School's under-achieving pupils are expected to conform with due deference and provide exuberant support at inter-school tournaments.

Perhaps this is where it all starts. From childhood we are encouraged to take an active interest and participate in Sport. This is a commendable ideal, especially in Australia, where the climate and conditions allow all year round sporting activity. However, as in all things, moderation is necessary or interest becomes an obsession and other more important issues are neglected or ignored. Then we are in danger of becoming ignorant and manipulated, like pawns on a chessboard; our minds and our judgement become clouded by a continual on-slaught from the Media, with sports news and the achievements of sporting heroes. Our complacent 'she'll be right' attitude is thus fostered and exploited by the cunning puppeteers in high places.

Otherwise, how did we ever allow the Banking Industry to become so profit-taking and self-serving? They are effectively un-fettered in their avaricious ambitions, in the way they impose unjustifiable charges for services that used to be freely offered. They impose their will on account holders by discouraging personal transactions over the counter and promoting the use of robotic ATM's and 'Phone-pay'.

Then they close a Branch that has served the Community for years, and funnel their customers to another larger Branch kilometres away, sack as many employees as they can and cut service to the degree where their customers are compelled to stand, waiting, in long queues. They boast about their obscene profits, while those in Government, with the power to legislate against their usury and exploitation and staff 'rationalising' do nothing.

How did we ever allow our Trade Agreements and this so-called 'level playing field' to reach a point where we can buy lemons and oranges imported from California, while our own orchards are being bull-dozed? How many factories in Australia still make electrical goods and appliances? Shoes? Clothing? Tools?

How did we ever allow our immigration policy to deteriorate to the situation where all sorts of recalcitrants, recidivists and other undesirables have established a firm foothold in the suburbs of our cities, controlling the distribution of narcotics and setting up prostitution, gambling and extortion networks.

How did we ever allow the shameful situation to develop, where the home telephone has become a luxury. Line rentals have escalated to a level that cannot be justified. Telephone services, like the Bank services, have become less efficient and more expensive, and Telstra, in the same manner as the Banks, boasts of its obscene profits while no questions are asked .... and the Government does nothing.

How did we ever allow successive State governments to implement the closure or reduction of our rail services, allowing the proliferation of heavy road transport to reach a stage where our highways are over-worked, under-maintained and downright dangerous. 'Without Trucks Australia Stops' is the popular axiom we often see on the rear of these multi-wheel juggernauts as they hurtle past. No argument there! It should not have reached this stage. There is plenty of freight movement to keep both road and rail transport on a viable basis, but the pollies and their advisory 'bean counters' figured there was more revenue to be gleaned from truck operators in various charges like registration, taxes and fines, while the railways could be relegated to the level, of a third world operation. Now, typically, road transport has become so competitive that many operators are either in financial difficulty, have already been bankrupted, or have been killed, trying to keep impossible deadlines and unattainable solvency.

Our complacency is how all of these abominations have been allowed to develop. 'She'll be right'. It's more important or socially acceptable, to care about who won the football, or the cricket score, or how we went at Wimbledon. Next time you are with a group, try starting a conversation about Banks, Trade Agreements, Telephones or Transport. Note how the group will disperse for all sorts of sudden reasons, only to reconvene at a discussion on Sport, in another part of the venue. Then, perhaps once in a generation when someone, for all the right reasons, wants to enter the rotten world of Politics, out of genuine concern for the future of our Nation, do we support that person? Sadly, as always, we allow the Media to embark on a campaign of denigration and vilification, while giving unlimited attention to the rabid cavilling of the do-gooders, the corrupt manipulators of the Establishment and those with a subversive agenda. Instead of: giving this person our respect and support, and rejecting the hostile propaganda, we turn our backs, sanctioning the deliberate attack on the democratic principle of freedom of speech and allow this person to become a victim of calculated vindictiveness and public indifference.

STOP BEHAVING LIKE SHEEP

Australians are becoming soft. Soft minded. Soft people are usually knocked over by hard people.' The quote is from David Foster, winner of Australia's highest literary honour, The Miles Franklin Award, in 1997, in Paul Sheehan's book 'Among The Barbarians— The Dividing of Australia'. To anyone who still has a brain, as yet un-befuddled by drugs and soft living, I cannot recommend this book highly enough, as it says it all. We have to wake up to ourselves and start challenging the misinformation too often fed to us by the media, and the decisions made to our detriment by politicians and bureaucrats.

It seems that the only ones who are prepared to make themselves heard and demand attention from the media and governments are the noisy, un-elected and un-representative minority groups. Why is it that the rest of Australia's population choose to remain sheepishly silent? Surely, in any democracy, an elected representative government is there to administrate for the good of the MAJORITY of the people. Time and again, however, laws and benefits are changed or introduced to suit any vocal and assertive minority section that can persistently attract enough attention from the media, until they get their own way.

For example, the Republic advocates. For no reason apparent to the majority of us, they suddenly started ranting, raving and complaining about the need for a change in our present system. They persisted in drawing attention to themselves until the media and the Government started taking notice of them. Never once were they able to demonstrate in any credible way, how Australia would benefit from becoming a Republic. Never once were they able to give a plausible explanation of how the great majority of us would receive a material advantage in any way. Was it going to improve our pathetic balance of trade, or do anything to reduce the National Debt? Would it mean a reduction in the number of un-employed? Did it offer any solution to the increasing problem of drug abuse and suicides, presently affecting our greatest asset ... our young generation? Would the enormous and increasingly urgent problem of adequate and equitable health care enjoy any benefit? Absolutely and positively NO.

Instead, their strategy was purely emotive and lacking in any logic. They carped about severing the ties of Colonialism, as if we were still living in the 1890's. They never acknowledged, for example, the fact that our legal system had done away with appeals to the British Privy Council, decades ago. They wanted to replace the Queen's representative, the Governor General,, with a President, whose function was ostensibly no different and certainly no less a burden to tax payers and offered no benefit whatsoever. They derided our beloved National Flag because it has a small Union Jack in the top left corner, as if it was the Sign of The Beast Where would they have us believe the First Fleet came from? Massachusetts? Finland?

Conveniently and deviously, they never mentioned the cost to the Nation's tax payers that the change would inevitably incur. Minting a new currency, removing all reference to the Queen on coins and bank-notes would necessitate making new dies on all the machinery. Any manufacturer will be aware of the great expense involved in a change of this nature. Then there would be the new Flag of the Republic After an expensively promoted competition for a new design, new flags will have to be manufactured and supplied to all government offices and the military. They even had the temerity to tell us that we have to remove all traces of our colonial past in order to gain respect and trust from our trading partners in Asia. What puerile rubbish! Then, of course, elaborate and lavish celebrations would be the order of the day. The victors would organise a huge party all at tax payers expense ... complete with a fireworks extravaganza, to which our triumphant leaders, both those we elected and those we did not, would attend. Foreign dignitaries would also be invited, along with the loyal and well-connected pro-republicans, who campaigned for the change. No expense will be spared to lavish food, drink and favours on themselves and the invitees and a jolly time would be had by all.

The hangovers would come later.

Fortunately, it hasn't happened ... yet. We had to have a referendum, however, before this baseless notion was defeated. The fact that a referendum was imposed upon the Nation at the cost of millions of dollars, for something totally irrelevant, only proved one thing. Too many of us behaved like sheep. Instead of being swept up in a wave of jingoistic emotion by this divisive and ill-founded call for a Republic, the majority of Australians should simply have stopped to ask why. What was the need for changing a system that was working perfectly well? More importantly, who stood to benefit? Had enough of us stopped to think, instead of being manipulated by a few with their own self-serving agenda and glib tongues, there would have been no referendum, no expenditure of millions of dollars, that could have gone to better use, and we could have been better off.

After the referendum and the Republic 'push' lost, did the sky fall in? Did any Asian Country refuse, thereafter, to trade with Australia? Did any foreign government threaten us with dire or serious consequences? In fact, hardly anyone outside of Australia took any notice. Which only goes to show what a great farce it was, and we were all dragged into it because we allowed ourselves to be led like sheep.

The tragic Port Arthur massacre in 1996 provided a perfect opportunity for another noisy minority to eventually force their will and their opinions on the rest of us. Hysterically blaming the weapon instead of the weapon bearer for this, and every other crime committed with a firearm since 1788, they effectively managed to bring about the disarming of the law-abiding citizenry throughout Australia. Now, everyone owning a firearm of any kind, apart from Police and military personnel, is assumed by these rabid, vocal extremists to be a mental case and a potential murderer. Two significant facts have emerged since. Firstly, while they may claim to have statistics showing a decline in the number of murders committed with a firearm, they cannot show any statistics that indicate a decline in the actual number of murders committed, overall. In other words, those with murderous intent have simply found other means, anyway.

Secondly, as it is said that locked doors only keep out honest people, similarly, the ban on firearms has only disarmed honest people. Criminals, by their own nature, recognise no laws anyway and still have access to firearms of practically any description, and use them whenever the occasion suits them. Thanks to the knee-jerk reaction by our politicians to the emotional outbursts and un-justified vilification of all gun owners by the anti-gun lobby, all intruders and gangsters possessing a firearm can feel much safer now, confident that their intended victims have no adequate means of defending themselves, their families or their property.

Conspiracy theorists have speculated that the Port Arthur massacre was a convenient and timely excuse for the leaders of both Federal and State Governments to disarm us all, to ensure against a future up-rising. If so, then we could wonder what type of secret agenda are they planning, that involves us all and makes them so apprehensive towards our reaction. It is thought provoking when one considers how the leaders of all States, despite their differing ideologies and politics, were so suddenly eager to get together, in such a short period of time, after the tragedy occurred, and reach agreement to impose such draconian legislation, without the usual procrastination and bickering so characteristic at any other time.

Again, this has been the result of the silent majority allowing themselves to be led like sheep, allowing their rights to be further eroded by the noisy, extremist minority. Every year, there are more people being killed on our roads than are killed with fire" arms. Should we ban motor cars? Has anyone proposed a ban on people with a mental problem from driving? How about a psychology test for all applicants for a Driver's Licence? Isn't it strange that all those who drive a motor vehicle are assumed to be mentally stable, while those who own a firearm are not! Lunatics in charge of motor vehicles can be seen on our roads, every day, and our leaders do damn all of any significance to disarm them. Instead they pay lip service to protecting the rest of road users by installing revenue-raising speed cameras and wasting the time of trained Police personnel by deploying them on random breath testing. While a miniscule percentage of motorists are caught "with a blood-alcohol reading above the legal limit, a much larger percentage are driving while under the influence of a narcotic, and nothing is done to protect us from them with any sort of testing.

If our leaders were more honest about addressing the problem it should be seen that most incidents are ultimately due to two causes; 1. Incompetence, and 2. Attitude. Incompetence can be largely addressed by more comprehensive training in defensive driving and vehicle control. Attitude can be assessed with a psychology test to determine a licence applicant's sense of responsibility and consideration for other road users. Offenders holding an existing license could be subjected to the same test to determine whether or not they should have it revoked. Bad attitude, for example, manifests itself in aggression, impatience, selfishness, in-attentive driving and driving while under the influence of alcohol or a drug.

The revenue raised from fees and fines should be used to fund these measures. It simply isn't good enough to use the issue of road safety as another cynical means of raising revenue for government coffers. Nor is it sensible to have trained law enforcement officers occupied on speed cameras and random breath testing congregations, involving several officers and a variety of police vehicles, when they should be better employed patrolling public parks and streets. If we can have Parking Police for enforcing parking regulations, why don't we have Traffic Police for enforcing traffic regulations?

All of us need to stop behaving like sheep, while the politicians do it all over us. They are there to serve our interests, not the other way around, as seems to be the way it is at present.

Another example of how we are being led like sheep is at the supermarket. If you read the small print on the package of each item before choosing it, you may be surprised at how many are imported, un-necessarily, in competition with an Australian made product, often on the same shelf. If we were to adopt a more negative approach in the way we shop, by avoiding imported goods when we can buy Australian, it would serve to keep our industries alive, and our own work force employed. It may be argued that while many of the products are made in Australia, the companies that make them are owned by foreign multinationals, but while they maintain a presence here, they are still employing Australian workers. However, if we buy shoes, for example, made overseas in some Country where wages paid to workers are extremely low, we are only helping the profit taking of retailers and foreign interests.

Price, of course, can be a deciding factor when people are on a limited income and a restricted budget, but when we look around at how many others can afford large, elaborate homes, expensive cars and exotic holiday destinations, it is obvious that not everyone is financially constrained. We all owe it to our country and our descendants to support Australian industries and farms wherever possible, before we wake up one day to find we have been completely sold out.

Earlier in this book, I made a reference to trends ... a perfect illustration of how so many of us are led like sheep, into adopting modes of behaviour and styles of dress, even though they may be denigrating, disfiguring or uncomfortable to those who embrace them. Blessedly, most of these affronts to our intelligence have a finite life span, and may be remembered in the future with some embarrassment by those former trendies whose maturity has eventually caught up with them. I imagine there will be a long waiting list of those who had indelibly etched tattoos on their bodies and ultimately wish to have them removed with laser treatment.

The massive adoption of 4WD (4 Wheel Drive) motor vehicles as the family car, however, is of more serious concern, due to the long term effect it is having on our consumption of fossil fuels, a finite resource, and our road accident rate. They are, in most cases, not purchased or used for the purpose for which they were originally designed ... . specifically on bush tracks, harsh terrain and severe conditions. Most of them never leave the bitumen, and in a great number of cases, are just an expensive, trendy mode of transport for mothers to take the children to school, and do the weekly shopping.

With their luxurious interiors, rainbow colours and over-powered engines, they have become the latest status symbol in our society, where our acceptability and social standing is measured, not by what we are, but by what we appear to possess. On the practical side however, they are notorious fuel guzzlers, expensive to maintain, and as recent crash tests have revealed, not as safe as their truck-like appearance might have their owners and occupants believe. Their rigid chassis construction, while adding to their weight, does not absorb impact as effectively as does the monocoque construction of the modern family sedan. In addition, their higher centre of gravity, due to their box-like configuration and large wheels, render them more susceptible to roll-overs on sharp curves or sudden changes in direction.

Where collisions are concerned, they are more lethal to the occupants of family sedans due to the fact that most 4WD's have larger wheels and tyres, which places their body-work, especially the bumpers, at approximately head height to those occupants. Combine this with the fitting of bull bars to flaunt a 4WD owner's macho egotism or aggressive disposition, and you have a potential weapon of serious destruction, ready to be unleashed on the unfortunate occupants of any sedan it happens to collide with, especially in a side impact. Many deaths and serious upper body traumas have occurred as a result, which would probably have been less likely, had the impacting vehicle not been a 4WD.

Another hazard created by these extravagant status symbols is in the way they obstruct visibility for the driver of the vehicle next to them. Try moving out into the traffic stream from a parking space when you have a 4WD parked next to you, on the side from which the traffic is approaching. It is like having a high wall blocking your view!

It seems that 4WD's and baseball caps have some psychological relationship or bond with their male owners. Where goes a 4WD, goes a male driver, wearing a baseball cap. The most significant message that this strange association implies is that the adoption of the two together is neither necessary nor motivated by any degree of intelligence.

Where female owners are concerned, it seems rather paradoxical for a petite, fashion-conscious and attractively presented member of the opposite sex to be seen perched at the wheel of a vehicle that has a resemblance more akin to a modified prime mover than a car. Perhaps this is another manifestation of their under-lying desire to be seen as equals? This was probably reflected in the comment heard from one woman, who stated that she owned a 4WD simply because she 'wanted to be a presence on the road'.

Referring back to my advocating a psychology test for licence applicants I rest my case!

POSITIVE THINKING PSYCHOSIS: THE CLIFF-HANGING MENTALITY

At the beginning of this book, I referred to the perils of positive thinking causing the denial of reality. Just as many people who attempt to climb vertical precipices, deny the irresistible force of gravity, to their ultimate detriment, the positive thinker who denies reality often suffers a similar fate. There will always be a precipice too steep, or an overhang too wide and there will always be positive thinkers who fail to recognise the limits and boundaries, beyond which their intrusion results in disaster.

The crucial factor is knowing when to stop. It is knowing when you have enough, or as some philosophers might say, taking time to stop and smell the flowers. If Napoleon had been content to rule France, instead of aggressively attempting to create an empire, he may have survived to a ripe old age. So too, the many thousands of others who became participants and finally the victims of his bellicose folly.

If Lt. Colonel Custer had been content with being lauded as a hero of the American Civil War and not thereafter tried to upstage his commanding officers at Little Big Horn, it is possible that he and the many members of his ill-fated regiment may have lived to enjoy their retirement.

If Adolf Hitler had been content with leading Germany out of The Depression and not embarked on ethnic cleansing and world domination, the resultant suffering of millions and the destruction of catastrophic proportions may have been avoided.

In contemporary times, as the gap between the rich and the needy is becoming more pronounced, a great many are becoming obsessed with material wealth and the ostentatious display of expensive possessions. This often results in all kinds of physical and mental disorders occurring among those in the competitive environment of business and commerce, as they drive themselves harder to keep on top, keep their competitors at bay, increase profits, expand their business, or continue to afford an extravagant life-style. In order to maintain their achievement graph on an upward curve, the stress becomes more pervasive in their lives until inevitably, if they refuse to face reality, something breaks down and they find themselves in poor health or divorced, or suicidal.

Is it worth it? Is the price paid for setting the psychological vaulting bar ever higher as each goal is reached, a justifiable cost? Would it not be wiser to abandon the ambitious and pernicious positive thinking syndrome at a stage when it is time to pause and enjoy the fruits of their labours? Take time to smell the flowers! Forget about keeping up with the Joneses and let the Joneses knock themselves out!

Who wants to be the richest man in the cemetery?

CONCLUSION

If the opinions and observations in this book attract attention from the Human Rights and Equal Opportunity Commission, then it proves that our democratic right to freedom of speech is either severely eroded, or more likely, completely non-existent in the 21st. Century.

For this, we can blame our politicians, past and present, for at least ratifying, if not causing the removal of the freedom that our forefathers fought and died for. Predictably, some people will disagree with my views; I have already categorised the most likely sources from which they will originate. They have the right to disagree, but they do NOT have the right to silence or crush anyone who does not share their views, or questions their motives.

Ultimately however, for these people to have such unjustifiable measures at their disposal, we have ourselves to blame for our complacency in the past. When we should have stood up, en mass and objected to what the politicians were doing, instead we engrossed the sports sections of the papers and switched our T.V. to micro-cephalic sit-coms and more sporting events.

As a famous philosopher once wrote, "A country usually gets the government it deserves."

www.ingramcontent.com/pod-product-compliance
Lightning Source LLC
Chambersburg PA
CBHW072106280526
45788CB00006B/2424